# THE BRAVEST YOU

# THE BRAVEST YOU

### Five Steps to Fight Your Biggest Fears, Find Your Passion, and Unlock Your Extraordinary Life

## Adam Kirk Smith

A TarcherPerigee Book

**tarcher**perigee

An imprint of Penguin Random House LLC
375 Hudson Street
New York, New York 10014

Copyright © 2017 by Adam Kirk Smith
Penguin supports copyright. Copyright fuels creativity, encourages diverse voices,
promotes free speech, and creates a vibrant culture. Thank you for buying an authorized edition of
this book and for complying with copyright laws by not reproducing, scanning, or distributing
any part of it in any form without permission. You are supporting writers and
allowing Penguin to continue to publish books for every reader.

TarcherPerigee with tp colophon
is a registered trademark of Penguin Random House LLC.

Most TarcherPerigee books are available at special quantity discounts for bulk purchase for sales
promotions, premiums, fund-raising, and educational needs. Special books or book excerpts also can
be created to fit specific needs. For details, write: SpecialMarkets@penguinrandomhouse.com.

Portions of this book appeared in different form on asmithblog.com.

Library of Congress Cataloging-in-Publication Data
Names: Smith, Adam Kirk, author.
Title: The bravest you : five steps to fight your biggest fears, find your
passion, and unlock your extraordinary life / Adam Kirk Smith.
Description: New York : TarcherPerigee, [2017] | Includes bibliographical references.
Identifiers: LCCN 2017003288 (print) | LCCN 2017013144 (ebook) |
ISBN 9781101993477 (ebook) | ISBN 9780143129899 (hardcover)
Subjects: LCSH: Fear. | Self-realization.
Classification: LCC BF575.F2 (ebook) | LCC BF575.F2 .S586 2017 (print) |
DDC 152.4/6—dc23
LC record available at https://lccn.loc.gov/2017003288

Printed in the United States of America
1  3  5  7  9  10  8  6  4  2

Book design by Elke Sigal

Best efforts have been made to locate source attributions.

While the author has made every effort to provide accurate telephone numbers,
Internet addresses, and other contact information at the time of publication, neither
the publisher nor the author assumes any responsibility for errors or for changes that occur after
publication. Further, the publisher does not have any control over and does not assume
any responsibility for author or third-party Web sites or their content.

*To my wife, Jasmine*
*You are the bravest person I know*

"The bravest are surely those who have the clearest vision of what is before them, glory and danger alike, and yet notwithstanding, go out to meet it."

—THUCYDIDES

# CONTENTS

Fear is bad and you should never fear. That's the message I walked away with after hearing some guy in church talk about fear when I was ten years old. I can remember the faux-wood-paneled walls, my colorful sweater, and the man's maroon sport coat, but most of all I remember him trying to look like a hero as he condemned the whole congregation for the fear in our lives. As he rattled on about the evils of fear and how cowardly we were for letting ourselves feel it, I felt more defeated with every passing minute.

This was because, growing up, I was painfully shy, and my default reaction to everything in life was to be afraid of it. I couldn't figure out how some people seemed brave and others, like myself, couldn't seem to find courage, no matter how hard they tried. Sure, I despised that I had adopted fear as my identity, but how was it possible for someone as cautious and reserved as I was *not* to be timid, as the speaker insisted? Well, I did the only thing I knew I could do—the only way I thought I could be brave: I stayed silent. For most of my childhood and adolescence, I didn't utter a word to anyone about my fears and instead held them inside, trying to put up a courageous front to everyone around me.

Walking around afraid all the time, and too afraid to say anything about it, left me paralyzed. I never talked about it with my parents because I wrongly assumed they would agree with the man's ideas and insist that I too should be able to deal with fear. I wanted to live up to their standards and, hopefully, make them proud. But after living this way until my late teens to early twenties and letting fear become a way of life, I eventually became exhausted. Something had to give. If I were to get anywhere in life, I knew I had to adjust my approach—or eventually those never-ending feelings of anxiety and dread would overpower any dreams I ever wanted to chase after.

Then something interesting happened. When I decided to stop letting some guy's negative message play on repeat inside my head and started thinking for myself, my constant feeling of alarm began to be replaced by curiosity and even hope. I discovered that when we challenge what others have said in the past, we stop their negativity from filling us with fear. When we turn away from negativity, the difference in our outlook shows up in our words, in our thoughts, and in the actions we live out each day. Shifting my perspective and looking past the lies that fear perpetuates absolutely changed my life, and it will do the same for you.

It was during this time that I began questioning everything I had learned in my younger years. I knew I needed to stop taking everything I was told as fact and to start finding out the truth for myself. When I became curious enough to start seeking some answers, I began to talk to others about the fears I was facing. Along the way, people also began opening up to me about their own fears. In fact, every person I talked to had something they feared, and I began to realize that maybe there wasn't anything wrong with me after all. When these people shared their fears with me it was beautiful vulnerability at its finest.

When I finally understood that fear was the one thing keeping me from fully connecting with people and giving more of myself to the world, I began to understand why the angry man who scolded us in church all those years ago was disgusted with fear. His message that had since haunted me was completely wrong—fear will come, it is necessary, and is many times an indicator that we are on the right track—but telling us to fight fear with everything inside ourselves was a message that we all need to hear.

We all have a responsibility to find bravery, because there are people who are waiting for us to fight our fears and to embrace our futures. Beyond the selfishness that keeps us looking after only ourselves, and the heartache we experience that keeps us fragile, and the busyness that tells us we just don't have time to worry about doing more with our lives, there are people who need to know that they're not alone with their fears.

Many people discount humanity with blanket statements like "people are too selfish to care," but as I look at the world around me, I know there is more to it than that. When people connect on an eye-to-eye and soul-to-soul level, the need to be brave in more situations becomes real. Therefore, to fight fear we must know that there are individuals who receive the benefit of our bravery for it to matter. That in itself is something to become passionate about, because people always matter.

It is this passion for people that draws us to one another, and it's the sharing of our fears that can create dialogue and understanding. To make a lasting impact on the world, this is something you must take to heart. Creating the truest form of community and relationship always requires both passion and bravery.

A passion for others and the belief that one can make a difference are at the foundation of every brave action. In fact, the only reason bravery is worthwhile is that it helps others. If you pursue bravery only to help yourself, then the connection to others that is deeply ingrained in each of us isn't fulfilled.

When you're only focused on yourself, your inadequacies seem to be glaring faults. When passion for others is your focus, the urge to be brave and to help people will always be more important than the fear that accompanies your imperfections. Whenever my focus has not been on others or I haven't believed that I could make a real difference in this world, instead of being brave I have chosen the easy way out. However, when you see that you serve a purpose that is bigger than yourself, putting in the necessary effort to find bravery always becomes worthwhile.

Think with me, for a minute, about how passion works. Before you act or even find courage and ways to act, at the heart of your being is passion. Sure, some people ignore passion, but that doesn't cancel out the fact that it's there. The individuals who do ignore it completely miss the fact they need passion and why they need to fight fear in the first place. Few people recognize passion for what it is—the fuel behind bravery. For the information in this book to stick with you, passion must be your drive. Consider this thought for a moment: A woman wants to write a book, and she realizes that the core reason she wants to write it is to help give others a greater understanding of the topic she is writing about, and to help others get through difficult experiences by relating to what the book is about. There has to be more in it for her than just worrying about writing a book. There are readers with real lives, real burdens, real troubles, and she can offer useful advice for them through her words. Through her passion her book can help bring hope to life. She may not even realize it yet, but it's there. Once she searches herself and discovers what she already has in her possession, she can use it to connect to others' lives.

If you think about how many people are on this planet, the odds are that you will run into someone who shares both the fears and passions you have experienced throughout your own story. We are not alone in our life experiences. Each of us can use this common ground to relate, to become closer, and to offer hope through passion for life and people. The people who make the biggest impacts with their lives do just that. When you grab hold of passion for yourself, you show others they can find passion too.

So how can we all become more aware of the role passion needs to play in our lives? We must ask the questions, "Why is this important?" and "Who will my actions impact?" Those answers are inside you already, but you must pay attention. When these answers are realized, fear becomes much less of a power in your life.

Everyone experiences fear, but very few are equipped to properly deal with it. This book will teach you a five-step process that helps you tackle and overcome the ten biggest fears you will face in your lifetime. Stop worrying about your other pursuits and begin to focus on the journey that bravery requires. Until you discover that you need bravery before you need anything else, you will live your life lost. When you find bravery, you find life.

## CHAPTER 1

# The Five Stages of the Bravery Process

At some point—present or past—fear has torn us all away from some significant accomplishment or victory. You can probably think back to a moment in life where you avoided it, suppressed it, or hid it. If your experience is anything like mine, I know that none of these reactions helped you achieve anything. Instead, you found yourself further away from what you wanted to accomplish and more frustrated than ever before.

But you don't have to keep running from fear. In fact, there's a way to overcome and eradicate each and every fear you face. Let me introduce you to the five-step bravery process I have created to help people fight the ten biggest fears we all face. The diagram below outlines its specific steps—or stages—which everyone moves through in their quest to unlock an extraordinary life: complacency, inspiration, fear, passion, and bravery.

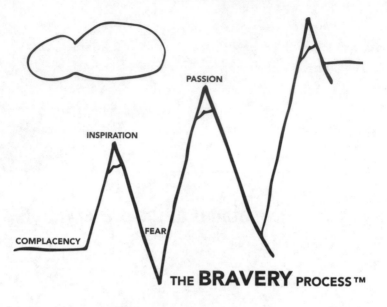

INSPIRATION

PASSION

COMPLACENCY

FEAR

THE **BRAVERY** PROCESS ™

Note that you start off at a low and flat point of complacency or the "playing it safe" stage, before an inspiration or idea strikes that spurs you to want to make a positive change. Often this is also the point at which one or many of the common fears we'll explore in this book sets in. You may find yourself asking questions like "What if I fail or am rejected?" "What if I'm not up to the challenge?" "What if it's the wrong decision or it ends up hurting my future or those around me?" These or unexpected obstacles can easily send you back into the valley of doubt and fear. But as I will show you in each chapter, you can harness the power of your passion and drive to overcome any fears or mental blocks that are stalling your progress toward achieving your dream. And eventually that leads to the final step of the process, bravery, where you emerge stronger and more courageous and confident than before. In undergoing this journey, you eventually move to a higher and much happier point in your life and toward the bravest version of yourself.

It's important to point out as well that I've placed the five stages of the process in this order because it is the order in which most people whom I have worked with as a successful business consultant and life coach—and many I interviewed for this book—have experienced them. I underwent them in this order as well. However, you may find that you go through them in a different sequence, perhaps with an idea or inspiration sparking your bravery process and then fear or complacency settling in until something kindles your passion and drives you to take the leap to achieve your goal. The order in which you undergo the stages doesn't matter as long as you keep moving toward the end goal, which is developing the courage to pursue what you want and live the life you've dreamed of. Along the way, you will be reminded of why you started climbing in the first place, and you will be forced to make the most important decision of your life, possibly more than once: choosing whether to give in to fear or fight it and climb onward toward bravery.

This book will help you power through your own bravery journey, so the critical first step is to identify where you currently are in the process. Let's start by exploring complacency, and then we'll move to finding ideas that are big enough to pursue and passion for them that is strong enough to carry you through to bravery.

## Complacency (the "Playing It Safe" Stage)

If you know anything about car racing, or sports for that matter, then you have probably heard of NASCAR driving legend Richard Petty. Many people remember him for his Charlie 1 Horse cowboy hat and trademark sunglasses, but he's best known for winning the Daytona 500 seven times. Something happened in the 1970s that sent his winning streak into a tailspin, though. His opponents changed with the times and updated their cars, but instead of doing the same, Petty was complacent. When asked how things changed so drastically, he answered: "We'd been winning steadily for twenty years and decided we wouldn't change." Petty played it safe, and as a result he didn't have one win in the last eight years of his career. Not one.[1]

Complacency and/or "playing it safe" are silent enemies that can tell us all the reasons why we don't need to keep pressing forward and become better. This concept doesn't just apply to sports—it can stall any aspect of life or business. As I mentioned earlier, I played it safe for such a long time that once I got an idea, I never looked back, but for many, the idea comes first in the bravery process, and complacency follows suit. Again, keep an eye out for this during your bravery journey.

If the word "complacent" comes to mind when you think about yourself, then you need to begin by asking yourself this two-point question: "How much is living a great life worth to me, and can I afford to not become better?" Your answers will give you your much-needed reason to begin moving away from complacency and toward bravery right now.

So what does "playing it safe" or "being complacent" look like? One way that people play it safe is by using their full schedules as a reason for why they aren't pursuing more of their life's dreams. As life becomes busy, we become attuned to the rhythm of monotony, and the easy thing to do is to let time get away from us. Chances are that a lack of time is the reason you fall back into this false sense of security and aren't adding more value to the world around you. This is why you will see many ideas around the subject of time in this book—our fears and our amount of available time are related in many instances. I get it. You are busy. But maybe your busy life is your crutch: you keep saying yes to things that don't matter, and that is what keeps you in the safe zone.

The problem is, life just keeps getting busier, and our crazy schedules will keep us stuck in a boring, safe routine. "Oh, my boss wants me to work such long hours that I only get four hours of sleep a night and barely see my family." Sure, gotta become a workaholic to make money and get it all done—right? Maybe you know what I'm talking about. If we're not careful, other people, or outside forces with their own agendas, will recruit us as their puppets. When we find ourselves letting everyone else dictate what we do and how we use our lives, we miss out on vital opportunities to succeed, grow, and feel fulfilled, ultimately leading to complacency. I know you don't want to give busyness the upper hand and bury the chance of moving forward with the life you want, and the good news is that you don't have to.

It's time to take back your life. Fix your schedule to create space. This much-needed time is what will get you to the next stage: ideas. I don't want you to find this space only for the sake of clearing out the mental clutter that bogs us all down. I want you to find more time before you begin moving, to allow you to tinker with ideas in the next stage. Having time not only allows you to think about what is ahead, but also frees you up long enough to really engage with your thoughts, put them under the microscope, and then test them out.

If you're having a problem with thinking of new ideas, your issue is probably not a lack of imagination; busyness is what's keeping you rushed and clouding your mind. Without rest, meditation, and free thinking, you will continue using the crutch of playing it "busy" and safe for far too long. Learning to fight busyness should be your number one priority. How do you do this? By focusing on what you want and need to accomplish.

When you know what your top priorities are, you don't have to wonder what needs less attention, because you have already stream-lined your life to focus on what matters most to you. Prioritizing brings clarity and direction. When you take on anything and every-thing, life quickly becomes chaotic. You can't possibly do everything and still do it well. But when you decide what you need to pour your heart into, you allow yourself to be more creative in those areas and can make a bigger impact with your life's work.

Now, grab a notebook and take ten minutes to write down your current priorities before you begin this journey. You will need this notebook for later exercises as well so keep it close by. (If you already know your priorities, use this prompt as a reminder.) Now that you're finished writing your priorities down, take a look at your findings. Are you happy or unhappy with your results? If you're unhappy with your priorities, the good news is that you can now make changes as you see fit.

But don't wait to remove what doesn't move you toward your goals. Make a phone call if you need to make a phone call to free up more time. Send an e-mail if you need to send an e-mail. Schedule a meeting if you need to schedule a meeting. Whomever you need to talk to and whatever you need to do to create more time in your day, do it right now. This book is pointless unless you take action to im-prove your life. Place a bookmark here and continue reading once you eliminate the unnecessary.

Now that you have your focused priorities, you can add more things back into your schedule. But as you add these commitments back in, you will now be more aware of your unique purpose. This step is so important because when you take the time to tweak your life to hold only what is near and dear to your heart, you become op-timistic and more effective with your efforts.

Great things happen when there is time to mold our ideas into better ones, and that only happens when we give the process of finding solutions more of our time. Rushing creativity leads only to basic, surface thoughts, but when we have time to ponder our ideas, we get to push through and dig deeper to find the best possible answers to our biggest questions.

Prioritizing helps us commit to what is important and lowers our unnecessary stress levels. Overwhelming stress is not helpful, but the kind of stress that moves us out of our comfort zone is not necessarily a bad thing. Stress is sometimes the little push we need to get things done, but again we need to make sure that the stress we are feeling is only being directed toward what is important enough to pursue further.

As each of us figures out our priorities, it's important to consider the season of life we are in. Not all life seasons are the same. Some are busier and some are slower, and it is your job to be aware of the season you are in and still affect the world in the midst of it. If it is a busy time in life, then your impact probably won't be as big. If you find yourself with tons of freedom, though, it's time to get to work. As I write this, my wife and I have two young children. I own two businesses and am involved in various community projects. But if you were to ask my wife how our marriage is, she would say it is the best it has ever been. How is this? I have learned how to manage time well. But if it were the old me, I would probably have to let go of the community involvement at least. It's about knowing your season, seeing your limits, being realistic with your time, and prioritizing what is truly important.

When I began the process of stepping out and deciding to not play life safe, did I bite off more than I could chew at some points? Did the pursuit of bravery and moving ahead sometimes cause me to commit to too many things? I have to answer yes, but it was because my focus wasn't on priorities. I kept agreeing to do more without looking at what was truly valuable. Again, to move from playing it safe your priorities need to be aligned to free up time so you can take on bigger and better things. And if you ever feel like you don't have enough time for your priorities and everything else in life, just remember the story of the mayonnaise jar and two cups of coffee.

A professor stood before his philosophy class, with some items in front of him. When the class began, he picked up a very large, empty mayonnaise jar and filled it with golf balls. He then asked the students if the jar was full. They agreed that it was. The professor then picked up a box of pebbles and poured it into the jar. He shook the jar lightly. The pebbles rolled into the open areas between the golf balls. He then asked the students again if the jar was full. They agreed it was, again. The professor then picked up a box of sand and poured it into the jar. Of course, the sand filled up everything else. He asked once more if the jar was full. The students responded with a unanimous yes. The professor then pulled two cups of coffee from under the table and poured their entire contents into the jar, effectively filling the empty space between the grains of sand. The students laughed. "Now," said the professor, as the laughter subsided, "I want you to recognize that this jar represents your life. The golf balls are the important things—your passions. Things that if everything else was lost and only they remained, your life would still be full. The pebbles are the things that matter, like your job, house, and car. The sand is everything else— the small stuff," he said. "If you put the sand into the jar first," he continued, "There is no room for the pebbles or the golf balls. The same goes for life. If you spend all your time and energy on the small stuff, you will never have room for the things that are important to you. So pay attention to the things that are critical to your happiness. Take care of the golf balls first—the things that really matter. Set your priorities. The rest is just sand." One of the students raised her hand and inquired what the coffee represented. The professor smiled and said, "I'm glad you asked. It just goes to show you that no matter how full your life may seem, there's always room for a couple of cups of coffee with a friend."[2]

This story shows you how priorities work, and I found it to work in my own life. I refused to say I didn't have enough time to do what I knew I was supposed to do. And if I didn't have enough time for my priorities, I knew my issue wasn't how much time I had but that I hadn't pinpointed my priorities well enough. If you want to move away from playing it safe, I have the exact same advice for you. When you identify your priorities, you are able to influence more people, meaning that you are able to pour more of yourself and your journey into the lives of those around you.

When you are able to offer more of your time to others, within reason, you open the door to increase your reach and your impact tremendously. I know you want to leave your own imprint on this world, and the solution is less selfishness, more giving of your available time, and hunkering down to do the work. In a way, holding back what you have to offer, by playing it safe, is a form of selfishness. It's keeping what you have from other people because of possible, but not probable, outcomes in order to play life safe. I know you don't want this for yourself, and I don't want it for you either.

Notice that you will never read a history book about people who stayed in the safe zone, and there's a reason for that. You can't make a lasting difference by playing life safe. It is in complacency that people keep to themselves, slog through a day at work, go home, and then do it all over again, without ever moving outside of their comfort zone. These are the same people who look up in disappointment or regret forty years later to see that their life has passed them by and there isn't much to show for their time.

You don't have to settle for being that person. Don't believe that garbage for one second. When you believe that you don't have to settle for mediocrity, you will begin moving ahead toward bravery and realizing your goals. Once you decide that you've been complacent long enough, you're ready to move to the next step: inspiration, where you will find or create the idea that will inspire you to stop playing it safe and start overcoming your fears once and for all.

## Inspiration (the "Ideas" Stage)

I remember watching Hello's Kickstarter campaign for the Sense sleep tracker in disbelief when it debuted. James Proud and his entire company were floored as well—their team exceeded its $100,000 goal and raised $2.4 million instead. Not only that, but Proud has since raised more than $40 million from other investors, totaling nearly $43 million in funding. The idea behind Sense is that it informs people of their sleep patterns and shows them what disturbs their sleep, so they can make corrections accordingly and get better sleep. Ultimately, this idea is helping people live better lives.[3]

Like Proud, I have had times in life when I look back at the journey I've just undergone and am immediately taken aback by what I was able to accomplish. Have you ever looked back on your journey and thought, "How did I just do that?" Well, it started with having an idea. You took it and shaped it and believed in it enough to follow through with an idea that you knew would somehow make a difference.

When you dream and give yourself permission to explore and release the ideas you've held hostage within you, for any number of reasons, it allows you to take the first steps toward living the life you've always envisioned for yourself but were perhaps too scared to try to make a reality. Realize that you have a chance to change something in your life, or make a difference in the world, and allow yourself to come up with new ways to do so. Whether they are little seeds of ideas that haven't fully formed yet, or audacious notions that don't seem obtainable from your current position in life, you can use this freedom to dream to your advantage.

In the inspiration stage of the bravery process, dream fearlessly, because this is the easiest and best time in the process to do so. The ideas you will find within you are hidden right now because you haven't taken the time to seek them out. But once you do, you will begin to find what it is that compels you to act on ideas. The decisions you make with these ideas will determine which direction your journey will go. Even if you don't feel like your ideas are the latest and greatest, don't let that keep you from talking about them or eventually carrying them out. The inspirations you have are there for a reason, and it is up to you to find why that is. No matter what idea you end up pursuing, it needs to be one that is big enough that it strikes a chord with you and will inspire you to face any number of obstacles without being discouraged and sinking back into complacency or fear. Almost anything that is important enough to pursue further will at first seem too big for you to handle, but keep moving. You'll get there.

These are the ideas that should be tossed into what I like to call the "idea-wrestling stage." I call it this, because we only wrestle with the ideas that we care about. If we didn't care, we would just drop them and move on. The idea-wrestling stage lets you rediscover yourself by seeking out what only you can possess, make better, and continue to grow in. Innovation is key to making your ideas grow. This is the spot where fresh ideas are born. When we don't wrestle with our ideas, we don't give them the chance they deserve. Holding ideas up to the light, analyzing them, tweaking them, testing them, and then repeating the process until the idea is where it should be, is how normal ideas are turned into great ideas.

What makes your idea unique is the fact that your story is different from everyone else's. Your experiences give you a different perspective on how ideas come to you, what they look like, and even the people you want to affect with your ideas. Perspective is one of the best tools in your arsenal, and you should use it to your advantage. Let your unique perspective influence your ideas and help move you toward bravery. It will even reveal the reason behind your need to pursue your idea. Your perspective is important because it reminds you that you have something unique to give the world, and only you can be the one to let it out.

Ideas frequently happen when the appeal of complacency starts to lose its luster. You may find yourself itching for a change or forced out of your element into a new and intimidating situation. The best question to begin with as you use your perspective to cultivate ideas is, "What would I do if I couldn't fail and I had all the time in the world to work on it?" What you have personally been through in life will give you your unique answers to this question. These answers will give you many opportunities, but that's what you want. Sure, it only takes one big idea to find bravery and use it to see huge results, but the odds of stumbling on the best ideas without wading through all the bad ones first is slim to none. The more ideas you come up with, the better the odds of finding that rare, life-changing idea that you will feel compelled to pursue further.

When people say they can't think of a single life-changing idea, I usually find that they aren't making much of an attempt to brainstorm them in the first place. You don't need to pressure ideas into forming; rather, let your various thoughts (no matter how seemingly silly or far-fetched) flow out, and write them down as you think of them. Let your life experiences and your passions speak to you. The more often you make time to do this, to learn from the life you are living, the more often you will be conscious of ideas that are trying to push through and make themselves known, and the more likely you will be to pay attention to them. Ideas come when you make yourself available.

The more you practice this idea habit, the more effortless it becomes to think of ideas and to let your brightest ones shine. With each attempt at this exercise, the ideas that you brainstorm will become better and better. And the more often you create them, the easier it will be to see which work and which don't. Listen to every idea that comes—whether five, fifty, or five hundred ideas—and record anything and everything that comes to you in your notebook. Why is writing ideas down so important? Statistics show that people who write down their ideas are much more likely to accomplish their dreams than those who don't write them down.[4]

Now, go ahead and cross out every idea but the three that resonate with you the most, that you most want to accomplish or pursue. Then number them in order of importance. Doing this will tell you which you need to tackle first. Once you home in on these initial ideas that move you to action, it will be time once again to do this exercise. The most fun part of this journey is seeing how life experiences change what you pursue.

Not only does coming up with these ideas require you to live more life, but at some point you will need to isolate yourself to give the ideas a chance to stick with you. Doing this also allows you to come up with a plan of action to turn your ideas into reality. Isolation tells me I should be spending time with people, but every creator knows that distractions take us away from our best creations. When we give our minds over to distractions, we end up giving less time to what is truly important. As a result, we fail to make the most of the ideas we decide to pursue.

Isolation is my least favorite part of the process. My family brings me more joy than anything else in this world, so why do I choose to isolate myself from them occasionally during this part of the process? Because it makes me a better visionary and ultimately a better husband, a better father, and a better provider. The more ideas I can come up with to achieve success in my work or other aspects of my life, the more I can share whatever rewards I reap with those I love and others around me. But I have to be careful here, and so do you. The important takeaway is to know that isolation is helpful only during the inspiration stage. To isolate oneself in fear is to head in the opposite direction from bravery. More often that not, when people isolate themselves in fear, they are lured back to playing it safe by the defeating voices that like to speak the loudest. You will know when it is time to disengage from isolation when you feel the momentum that comes with a new belief in yourself and an idea worth pursuing to the next stage. When you believe that you are the only person who can turn your idea into action, you will become even more committed to the bravery you need to accomplish your dreams.

Naturally, removing yourself from isolation will make you better in other ways too. At this stage, you need not only to create relationships to increase your life experience and perspective, but to make sure your idea is solid enough to withstand the journey. Dealing with this here ensures that you won't have to later. Relationships let people in and allow them to challenge your current position in life. My true friends, the ones who genuinely care for me, always have questions about the journey I'm taking, and this might be the most beautiful part of any relationship—caring. Deep relationships spark a community of creation and caring.

We all need this helpful balance during the inspiration stage, to help push us through fear. As weird as it might sound, we all need isolation, as well as relationships, to cultivate remarkable ideas. The inspiration process needs both if bravery is to become possible. Isolation helps us push forward because it is in the creation process that ideas come to life, but relationships are what give fuel to the flame of creation.

We find ourselves drawn into bravery when we have an idea that is so amazing that we aren't the only one who can rally around it. We need ideas so big that a community wants and needs to help push us further than we've ever thought possible. This means that the needs of other people can and will influence your work. This is important on a personal level but also if you ever want to provide a product or service to help individuals realize their own potential and succeed. It isn't enough to just have an idea; you need an idea so big that it will change the perspective of other people and their life's course. Make space, set priorities, and spend some time alone to know who you are and what you need to pursue, and to protect yourself from naysayers along the way. These people will appear, but when you know what your priorities and top ideas are, your intended path is clear and the negative voices become less of a distraction.

You probably already have an idea so big that it may feel weird to tell other people about it or even to say it out loud to yourself, but that's when you know it's a big enough idea to pursue further. Maybe you used to get these ideas and keep them hidden, because that's what you do if you want to turn around and go back to playing it safe. But you are better than that and hopefully are beginning to see your own potential.

No, the inspiration process won't be easy, but I don't know of many life-changing ideas that come without intense effort. In this stage it helps to realize that you still have time ahead of you and that it will take time to pursue the ideas you want to complete in your lifetime. As much as you want everything to happen right now, all at once, it can't and it won't. The lie of instant gratification will send you right back to the complacency stage, where if you're not careful, you will likely find yourself feeling stuck and unfulfilled again.

(A quick side note: Patience truly is a virtue that will be developed during the bravery process. You want it and you need it. More often than not, you will be able to push forward two steps but will end up taking one step back. That's why all of our journeys are a process. This is okay, though. If we keep taking two steps forward and only one back, we are still making progress. Slow progress, but progress nonetheless. This is why it's less important to focus on the timeline and more important to recognize the long-lasting impact your brilliant ideas can have.)

It takes more than a spark of inspiration or a great idea to make a positive impact, though. Once you have the idea that demands your attention and won't let go, fear will likely be your next reaction. You need courage to take your ideas beyond your fears. But if you can combine your brilliant thinking with enough bravery to overcome any fear that's holding you back, you will be unstoppable. And that's what we'll explore next—the fear stage of the process.

## Fear (the "I Can't Do It" Stage)

Franklin D. Roosevelt was the thirty-second president of the United States. He took office at the worst moment of the Great Depression and helped the American people regain faith in themselves. He truly was one of our greatest presidents, which is why he served four terms, from 1933 to 1945, as commander in chief of the United States of America.

In 1921, when he was vice president of a financial firm, Fidelity & Deposit Company, he contracted polio, a terrifying and incurable disease that left him paralyzed in his legs. He dealt with the disease all the way through his presidency, but his struggle was kept from the public eye. It was only through the challenging rehabilitation process, and with the support of his wife and his family, that Roosevelt was able to regain some use of his legs. Though polio devastated FDR physically, his determination only grew stronger as he fought through his recovery. His wife, Eleanor, later said of this time: "I know that he had real fear when he was first taken ill, but he learned to surmount it. After that I never heard him say he was afraid of anything."[5]

Now, am I telling you this story to compare your fears with the challenge of having polio or being paralyzed? Absolutely not, unless you are indeed dealing with one of those difficulties. However, I am saying that we can use tragedy to help us push through fear and reach our full potential. Life may bring us tragedies, and will certainly give us many reasons to fear, but we can turn these moments into opportunities to gain more insight into how fear works and how we can overcome our fears. Roosevelt was able to turn tragedy around and learn from it, and as a result became stronger through the experiences he was forced to face. He is best known for what he said during his first inauguration as president, in 1933: "The only thing we have to fear is fear itself."

In a time of severe economic crisis, it is no coincidence that Roosevelt led the nation with those powerful words. Being able to move through fear is what made Roosevelt the man he became. He became stronger and wiser from traveling a difficult journey. Fear can sometimes seem so big that we don't want to look at the situation at hand and instead run away, because we fear the fear itself—a situation Roosevelt understood and articulated so well. Fear is the biggest obstacle you will ever face in life, and not acknowledging fear only makes it stronger.

Maybe the fears you are facing aren't life-threatening like some that Roosevelt faced, but you can still see the principles that worked in his life and apply them to your own. You either learn to stand up to your fears and face them, or you fear the fear itself and head back to safety. As you can see, fear isn't necessarily a choice that will destroy you, but it will detour and detain you. It will keep you procrastinating for way too long if you let it, and will keep you from living out your own bravery journey.

In my own life, the thoughts I used to have from fear would blow situations out of proportion before I even got to the moment when I would begin the work. When this happened, I experienced just how powerfully my mind could exaggerate the circumstances at hand, and I gave fear the upper hand instead of giving bravery a chance. Whether my fears would tell me that I wasn't prepared enough, or wasn't smart enough, or wasn't good enough, I let fear take the leading role. Far too often fear told me all the reasons that I couldn't because I didn't allow for bravery to tell me all the reasons I could.

When you discover what it feels like to be able to push through fear, the thought and feeling of going back to it will disgust you. You already know that my struggle with fear affected me for many years, but I refuse to let it control me any longer. I found that I was tired of not accomplishing more with my life, and of letting fear and doubt constantly win. I was exhausted with running away from opportunity. I knew I needed to accomplish more, and I knew that it was a mental battle I had to win before I could go any further.

The fearful circumstances we encounter are the greatest menace we will ever experience, but when we choose to learn from them, we deny fear permission to antagonize us, and in return doubt doesn't get the chance to become a bigger factor in our lives. Now, take ten minutes to identify your top fears and write them down in your notebook, so you will constantly be reminded of them. This is important, not only because looking at your fears more often helps you become comfortable facing them, but you will need this list later. You need to be able to look back and see how you fought to find bravery in what currently seems like hopeless situations. Hopelessness comes when you feel you can do nothing about fear, but fear is never hopeless. Please know that. Don't let this list taunt you with the pain it can evoke; instead let this exercise be your beginning of hope.

This exercise reveals half of the battle with fear: acknowledging what you are afraid of and realizing that fear will come again, so you can prepare for it. When I did this exercise, it helped me realize something. I discovered that fear is part of the bravery journey. I came to terms with the fact that I couldn't eliminate fear, but I could encounter it, face it, and move through it, and you can too.

Listen, if your goals and dreams don't scare you, they're probably not big enough. Here's the part that the man from church in the story I shared in the introduction missed: fear will not only be a guaranteed part of your life—whether you like it or not—but it *should* be a part of your life. It doesn't matter how hard you try to escape fear, you will eventually face the choice of pushing forward to bravery, or giving in to fear and slipping back into complacency and, likely, unhappiness. Many things in life will scare you, but you must find ways to make it through fear, while learning many lessons along the way. This might immediately make you fear the thought of fear, as Roosevelt warned us we may, but we must learn to face fear in order to become better at living our lives to the fullest. Stop trying to avoid it, and embrace it instead.

Here's the kicker: When I realized that there is no way to avoid fear, I found liberation. But I knew there was still a very important decision to make. Would I simply cower in most scary or intimidating situations I encountered, or would I do something big enough with my life to make bravery worthwhile? To be totally honest, I became tired of harboring fear more often than feeling bravery, and that alone caused me to begin moving in the right direction. If nothing else, getting fed up with the fear you are facing can propel you forward.

I know you have huge plans for your life. You want to affect people, you want to change this world, and you want to make a difference. But, even after you decide this, life still happens and fear and doubt still come. It's what you do with this fear that determines whether you find bravery or stay stuck, but strive to not make fear a long-term option. Instead, begin seeking the reasons why you do what you do. Finding your motivation will help you move more quickly toward the things that once struck fear in your heart.

The "false evidence appearing real" (FEAR) in your mind is probably linked to negative consequences from actions you have taken in the past. This is because our memory can take us back to those vivid moments and force us to remember how we felt during and after them. This is especially true when we visit the same opportunities and attempt them again, to attain different outcomes. Fears like to associate themselves with particular feelings or situations and tell us to be uncomfortable when we see, feel, or hear about them. Action is the only thing that can cancel out fear of possible outcomes and bring our perspective back to reality. And the main reason most of us haven't taken action is that what we are going after isn't enticing enough.

When you decide to view fear as an indication that you're heading in the *right* direction, you use fear for good, as a stepping-stone, instead of looking at it as a roadblock. When you grab hold of this revelation in your own life, you will see that the things you are most fearful of are usually the same ones you are most passionate about. Fear likes to test us to see if we are really committed, but when we decide to answer back with action, our passion for this world and making a difference gets set in motion. And once you decide to fight back with your love for life and taking action, your passion will push you through to bravery.

Even if some of the fears you are holding on to are considered "universal," you probably learned to fear those things from somewhere or someone else, and to react accordingly. Whether in negative words spoken by others, your parents' lofty standards, or the feeling that a risk is too daunting to take, you will encounter fear in your lifetime and will need to be able to look past those things to choose bravery. Fear wins out when we believe that the consequences of our mistakes matter more than the right action. When you let fear win out, you are saying that avoiding fear is more important than the possible impact your ideas could have. Whenever you aren't able to move through fear and find everything that's waiting for you on the other side, you miss another opportunity.

Sure, life can get scary when we risk what we have and put ourselves out there, but what is life without fear? A life without fear is boring and won't change history for the better. If you are familiar with hiding from fear, then your first thought is probably, "Yes, Adam, my life may be boring, but it's not hectic." True, but boring doesn't accomplish much of anything. Boring doesn't change the world. Boring doesn't even need bravery. Yes, turning around and not fighting fear may feel easy in the moment, but it won't get you anywhere. Maybe you think that playing it safe and living a boring life sounds great because you won't have as many responsibilities, but if you want to change the world and make it a better place, then finding bravery becomes your main responsibility.

So what will help us move toward bravery more often than fear? Realizing that we have a choice about which internal voice we listen to. Fear is there in every situation you will ever find yourself in, but so is the option of pushing forward to bravery.

The paralimbic cortex and the amygdala have much to do with how we assess fear—both playing a role in conditioning and our emotional state—but it is the reticular activating system that regulates the processing of sensory information. This network of nerves takes its cues from the information we feed it—the voice of fear or the power of passion moving us toward bravery. This shows that we can begin training our brains to interpret fear as momentum, a positive stimulus rather than a setback.[6] When you take the time to train your brain correctly, and then pay attention to what you feel in individual circumstances, you will see whether you more often give in to fear or pursue bravery. The feelings triggered by fear will typically let us know we are on to something good, but we should also know to proceed with caution. To fight fear properly isn't to go for all or nothing and live life blindly. To tread wisely when fear arises is to take all possible influences into consideration, and then to use your smarts to act intelligently.

As you navigate the bravery journey, take notice of the moments that move you toward bravery. What were you doing to help you fight fear? What was your mental state in those times? Who were you surrounded by that helped you keep going? What were you thinking when you were able to push through your biggest fears? Those four questions will give you some extremely helpful insights about how you respond to the bravery journey. If we take notice of the world around us as we find success, we will always find teachable moments to help us form better judgments in the future. This is what it means to never waste a moment of your life. There is so much we can take away from being able to push through fear. The question is, have you taken the time to learn?

But what about all the times you chose fear over bravery? Will you stay in the past and only focus on those moments, or can you begin to move ahead? Stop beating yourself up over all the times you missed the mark. When you quit focusing on moments in the past when fear won—except to learn what not to repeat—you can give the big and small victories your bravery has enjoyed, and will in the future, the attention they deserve.

It is great to learn from the mistakes you make along the way, but it's more important to understand that you don't have control over the past. The only aspects of the past you control are your perception of it and the lessons you can learn from it. What you have the most control of now is what you will do with today and tomorrow. You can change the hold your past has on you by fighting the fears you are facing right now. Your past doesn't have to repeat itself. You can make your future brighter by the decisions you make today.

On most occasions, bravery must be sought out; it won't just find you. I wish it was that easy, but, again, discovering bravery is a journey, and sometimes a painful one at that. Research has actually proven that fear triggers the same part of the brain that responds to some pains.[7] That's why it hurts so much and can influence you to turn and run the other way when the going gets tough. Is pain a deterrent? Sure. Should you give in to a painful journey? Well, that's why it is so important to form an idea that's big enough to entice you to keep moving through each of the stages, knowing beforehand that it won't be easy. Don't kid yourself by thinking it will be easy, because that mind-set is setting yourself up for many upsetting surprises along the way.

To choose wisely in the fear stage, it helps to know some facts about fear itself. Researchers at the University of Cincinnati found that an astounding 85 percent of the things we worry about never even happen.[8] Also, 30 percent of things feared happened in the past and can't be changed, and 90 percent are considered to be insignificant issues.[9] These percentages show that if we give in to fear and fall into these averages, we will get to the end of our lives with a whole lot of wasted time on our hands.

How many times have you feared something and actually asked yourself, "What's the worst that can happen?" If you take the time to evaluate the consequences of acting out the things you fear, you will find that only very rarely will the possible results be detrimental to the final outcome of a project, dream, or goal. These are the unnecessary fears that it would be very wise to identify and to begin to spend less brainpower on immediately.

After picking through your fears and weeding out the unnecessary ones, ask yourself what your true fears look and feel like. They feel awful—don't they? When you give in to a legitimate fear, an immediate feeling of disappointment arises, because for some reason you weren't able to stand up to it with the excitement of bravery. You cowered away in fear, leaving you to feel powerless. Maybe you feel trapped by repeatedly giving in to your fears. When you're stuck in fear, you feel helpless, whereas on the other side of fear, a mind-set of "I can do anything" takes over. When you choose to fight fear, confidence comes as part of the package.

People who find themselves stopped abruptly by fear are usually there because they can't find confidence. They don't have enough reason to move past comfort, and instead of finding bravery they retreat quietly to safety without putting up a fight. These individuals sometimes play it safe for years on end, until they decide to tiptoe out and begin the journey once again. If this happens to be you, know that however long you decide to stay in the safety zone, you are wasting precious time.

A brilliant step to take when making any decision is to use your intelligence to evaluate the situation at hand and decide if it's worth the risk to move ahead or better to put your time and energy elsewhere. Passion alone is futile, but knowledge paired with passion changes everything. Realize that there is a big difference between choosing to play it safe because you don't have the confidence to push through fear and choosing not to push through fear because you decide the risk isn't worth your time. The former requires serious thought and evaluation, and the latter that you move on with what you're passionate about.

To even further help you with the decision making process, here are three reasons for you to keep moving forward, despite the risk:

- **If you can impact a person in a way that changes their outlook on life and helps change their course for the better, then it is worth moving forward.** This can be as big or small an act of empathy and kindness as you care to take. It requires positivity to change a negative outlook, and the person who can offer that is you.

- **If it moves you closer to developing a relentless passion for something you truly care about, then it is worth pursuing.**
  The more often you care, the better your outcomes will be.
- **If it moves you closer to achieving the courage required to attain your ultimate goal, then keep moving ahead.**
  Anything and everything you can find to help increase your self-confidence to move you toward bravery is a win.

To summarize these points succinctly, here's an equation you can use anytime you are contemplating whether a goal or ambition is worth the risk. If it meets the requirements on the left side of the equal sign, it's worth pursuing:

---

**Helping others + Moving you toward your passion and goals = The ideal pursuit**

---

If the idea you are chasing doesn't meet the criteria in the equation above, you're wasting your time and would be better off cutting your losses and moving on to something that fits. On the other hand, if you think you can find reasons to keep moving once you build up your confidence on the journey, it is always worth the wait to hold on to your dreams and choose to make your huge acts of bravery later on. Whether you need some time to make the better choice or you are ready for bravery in this moment, take the time to see just how committed you are to the journey. It may help to bite off fear in smaller chunks rather than fully committing to tackling your biggest fears today.

Maybe your biggest fear at this moment is about starting a business. You don't have to sign a lease for a storefront right now. But you should begin talking to other entrepreneurs, to gain insight on what it takes to own a business, which is what will move you toward your passionate dream of becoming an entrepreneur yourself. This is exactly what a woman named Holly did. She sought advice from me on her shoe store concept before grand opening day. She didn't have experience with footwear, let alone retail, but her passion to help residents of her hometown with a new business idea won out, pushing her to chase bravery with her new business venture.

You might fear owning a business right now, and that's okay. It's the daily action of living out your passion that will normalize your biggest fears. If you let it, the fear you feel will tell you to abandon all logic and return to safety, but bravery cultivated correctly is smarter than this. Remember that small steps made over time will still eventually bring you to bravery, but it is called a bravery *process* for a reason. Your final destination won't be seen tomorrow, but the point is that you are leaving fear behind with every step.

It's a good idea at this point to assess where you are in life and whether you are closer to fear or bravery in your journey. Take the current fears you identified in the exercise above and rate them on a scale of one to five, with one meaning you feel you could push through the fear today and five meaning fear strikes you to the core just to think about it. The key to this exercise is to get all your rated fears out where you can see them, so you will be able to understand how afraid you really are but also how committed you are to carrying each item out. This clears out what you don't really want to pursue, and gives you your bravery priorities.

Next, go ahead and dream about what it would mean for you to be on the other side of fear in all the bravery priorities you just identified. This exercise gave me a focused mental picture of turning my own dreams into successes, because I was finally able to see how close I was to surpassing the fears I rated as ones. The fears I rated as fives were still there, because I was committed to them, but identifying them allowed me to create specific steps to help me accomplish what I was most afraid of. Doing this exercise will help you begin moving in the right direction, just like it did for me.

It doesn't matter if you are an artist, employee, manager, or entrepreneur who wants to become more than what you are right now; if you can't see past your fears, you will always fall short of your true potential. If you have been waiting your entire life to step out and reach that potential, don't let feelings of inadequacy dictate the outcome. If you are an entrepreneur who is fighting the fear of failure, it may take risk to grow your business. Maybe you are an artist who isn't pursuing your life's work because of the fear of rejection. Maybe you fear change in this moment, but not all change is bad. Actually, rarely is change bad. Or maybe you don't want to give up what you currently have, because you are fearing the loss of control. Or maybe you fear the judgment of others about the adventure you are about to embark on, and that is keeping you from moving forward. But we must keep moving ahead to see what we are truly capable of, especially in the midst of fear.

Fear is an indicator that you are heading toward bravery and you just haven't found the benefits of it yet. Fear comes right before success might be realized. It is then that fear broadens its shoulders and looks its biggest, but it only appears that way. Stop viewing fear as something bad and begin seeing it for what it is—an opportunity. You may not be able to change your current situation, but you can change your current perception.

The key to moving ahead is to stop giving mediocre excuses as to why you can't fight fear and be the person you truly want to be. You know the excuses I am talking about: It's too late to begin. I'll do it someday. I'm not an expert. I'm not old enough. I'm not young anymore. I don't have the money. I don't have any time. I need to be ready first. It needs to be perfect. It's too difficult. Et cetera.

When the excuses begin to come, you must make a mental shift and see how much bravery is worth to you. When you focus more on the positive outcome that fighting your fears can bring, you can stop giving in to excuses and turning up the volume on negativity.

Your life is reflective of every excuse you make and every decision you don't. When we get to the end of our lives, the only thing that will matter is what we did with it. I want to be remembered for giving it my all—fighting fear with everything in me, holding on to passion, and relentlessly pursuing bravery. This is what it truly means to live life with purpose.

If you want your life to bring value to the world around you, you need to begin making decisions that push you toward bravery rather than making excuses that take you back to complacency. When you are able to stop making excuses, and instead begin taking steps toward bravery, your outcomes will line up with what you actually want from life.

As I think about the many excuses that people make for why they can't see bravery realized in their own lives, I am also reminded of the stories of individuals who could have easily made excuses but chose not to. Kyle Maynard's is one of those amazing stories. He was born without arms or legs, yet Maynard has done more than most people I know who have all their limbs intact. Of course he experienced fear along the way, but his passion to inspire others rang louder than his fears. He has set records in weightlifting, has become a championship wrestler, is the world's first quad-amputee mixed martial arts (MMA) fighter, is a *New York Times* bestselling author, and is now the first quad amputee to reach, without the aid of prosthetics, the 19,340-foot summit of Kilimanjaro. As Bernie Goldberg, an *HBO Real Sports* correspondent, said, "Kyle's taken away the right to complain from the rest of us."[10]

Kyle Maynard's life is an inspiration because he fought his fears, remained persistent, and created his own outcome. He could have easily made excuses and lived a normal life to anyone's standards, but he decided to live exceptionally with the cards he was dealt. He began writing his story and never looked back, and his journey is now making a difference in the lives of others. You too can fight fear and follow passion to have a lasting impact on others, but reaching bravery requires abandoning excuses and increasing determination.

If you think about every great moment in history, each was preceded by fear, but the difference between history makers and space takers are that the people who make history find a way to push through fear. They are committed to finding a way no matter what, and their purpose is big enough to take control of the situation. In a way, the ability to overlook fear and see what is waiting for them on the other side is what makes people great. They realize that there is more at stake than personal fear and shying away. They see the change that could, and will, take place from their actions alone, to change the lives of others. You have the same exact opportunity in your life. Want to create a great legacy? You will be remembered for the fears you fought and the fears you didn't. When you dare to discover bravery through fear you will begin making a difference in the world.

No, you won't learn to conquer fear once and for all, but that's life. On the bright side, the fact that you chose fear once doesn't mean you have to choose fear in the future. Some situations just take longer to figure out, and that's okay. Throughout life, you will need to constantly apply this process of finding bravery, because new fears will come. For the rest of your life you will be confronted with fear in various situations, just like everyone else, but you can be one of the few who can continually pass through it, to go on to bigger and better things.

## Passion (the "I Can Do It!" Stage)

"Passion" is a word some feel is overused, but it is the word that best describes the internal drive that moves one forward to bravery. Passion and bravery are linked, being that both start with one's heart. "Courage" comes from the Latin word *cor*, meaning "heart," and "passion" from the Latin *passio*, meaning "to endure." When we are passionate, we are willing to endure, even when quitting seems like the only option. Passion happens when you see the light at the end of the fear tunnel. It's the light in the darkness that will increase your willingness to push through fear and find bravery. Passion has a way of continually finding bravery through action, no matter the odds. This actually reminds me of a story I heard a few years ago, and I want to share it with you here:

A young violin prodigy was walking down the street one day, trying to decide whether or not to pursue a life in music, when he came upon the most famous violin teacher in the world. Scarcely believing his luck, he stopped the great teacher and asked if he could play for him, thinking he would abandon his dream of a career in music if the great teacher told him he was wasting his time.

The teacher nodded silently for him to begin. So he played,

beads of sweat soon appearing on his forehead, and when he finished, he was certain he'd given his finest performance. But the great maestro only shook his head sadly and said, "You lack the fire."

The young musician was devastated. He returned home and announced his intention to abandon the violin. Instead, he entered the world of business and turned out to have such a talent for it that in a few short years he found himself richer than he'd ever imagined possible.

Almost a decade later he was walking down another street in another city when he happened to spot the great teacher again. He rushed over to him. "I'm so sorry to bother you," he said, "and I'm sure you don't remember me, but I stopped you on the street years ago to play my violin for you, and I just want to thank you. Because of your advice, I abandoned my greatest love, the violin, painful as it was, became a businessman, and today I enjoy great success, which I owe all to you. But one thing you must tell me: how did you know I didn't have what it takes? How did you know all those years ago I lacked the fire?" The great teacher shook his head sadly and said only, "You don't understand. I tell everyone who plays for me they lack the fire. If you had the fire, you wouldn't have listened."[11]

**Passion is the irrepressible drive inside you to do something positive or great that will leave a lasting impact on yourself and, more important, on other people.**

Fighting for passion doesn't mean that you need to yell from the rooftops, but rather, it is an internal drive to succeed. Most people stop pursuing passion because of their preconceived idea of what passion is. It doesn't mean that you need to yell at the top of your lungs with excitement all day, every day. In fact, that's called being crazy, not passionate. Of course, everyone expresses passion in different ways, but sometimes the mental picture of what passion looks like can deter people from ever wanting to pursue it. Passion is and always will be the force that pushes you forward to find success—nothing more, nothing less.

Let's say that you started a business ten years ago and have lost a passion for what you are doing. I have met entrepreneurs in the tech industry, in the restaurant industry, in the footwear and apparel industry, in finance and so many other industries, who once had a passion for what they were doing, but are now living life without the passion that they once knew. On the other hand, I have also met individuals who have found their passion once again, and can actually voice that this is the reason they are finding success. Two reasons that they are finding success are that passion not only produces endurance and ultimately bravery, but passion also naturally draws other people in, and this can only help build better personal and business relationships. People want to have relationships with and work with people who genuinely care. People need passion because it is what connects me to you, you to me, and us to the rest of this world. When the first person told me that this was their difference maker, I didn't pay attention to it, but after hearing the thirtieth person say that passion was their reason for success, I started taking notice. There had to be something to this fact, and I began connecting the dots between passion and success.

Passion is the most useful tool in your arsenal and the hero of this story, because it is the fuel behind the work. But even more than having passion for the work we do, we must look at passion as something we need in our lives as a whole. The reason that so many people don't live life with passion is that they only look for passion within their work, never looking to make it a way of life. Of course finding passion in work is important, because the average person will spend eighty thousand hours working in their lifetime. I'm clearly not asking you to neglect that pursuit. But instead of searching passion out in the one area of life we tend to most focus on, we must search it out in every area of our lives.

Life is full of moments when you decide either to retreat or to go and do something with the passion you feel for life and for others. In life, there isn't really much "staying" involved. There is only retreating or moving ahead. If you think you are staying still, you are really retreating, because if you aren't moving closer to something, then you are losing good momentum and giving in to fear. If you aren't finding passion in what you're doing, stop wasting time retreating. Life is too short to live without passion for everything that life has to offer. When you find passion, moving ahead will be the only thing you can do, because it has a way of moving you forward on its own. And the only way your ideas will come to life is to put convicting passion behind them.

Everyone comes to this point of staying fearful or following what they feel compelled to do. It's a true crossroad in life. I love having discussions about the dreams and ideas people have and learning what brought them to that crossroad. A common question in these discussions about people's ideas and fears is, "How exactly do I find passion, Adam?" It's an extremely important question, because with passion you will feel compelled to fight your fears and finish what you started. I'll answer this question with five more questions you must ask yourself. Your answers will help you find your passion and learn how to incorporate it into your life, both personally and professionally.

### Question 1: How Are You Pursuing Your Biggest Passion(s) Right Now?

Passion works because it leads to a healthy obsession, and when anyone is obsessed with something, they won't stop until they find the answer they are looking for. Some people settle for something they like, but they don't continue along the journey to really find what they love to do and what they are passionate about. It requires a constant checkup, to see where you are with your pursuit. Take time to look around and see what this world has to offer. Find what you have been searching for, fight through fear to get to passion, and thrive.

### Question 2: What Would You Gladly Do for Free That People Want and Need from You?

I ask this question because there's no better way to narrow down options than asking people what they would do for free. Sometimes the answer is "nothing," and if that's you, no worries—question three is a good one, too. But if you enjoy volunteering your time in a specific area, it probably indicates that you are very passionate about what you are doing.

Answering this question can do two things: it really gets to the heart of what you are passionate about and your answers will help you find out what you're an expert in. When you decide to make passion a way of life, you will discover who you are and what you can offer to the world. When you put passion and people at the forefront, and not dollar signs, you will make better decisions and be better able to know the best reason to find passion and fight fear. This is a necessary, selfless question because we have become a society in which something is always expected in return. But what if the reward was found in truly living out what you are passionate about? Holding the answer to this question close to heart will help you live a passionate life. If you would do a lot of different things for free, then keeping those options available is what will eventually reveal your truest passion.

When you find what, out of the many, interests you most, and narrow it down to find your truest passions, you will finally discover your deepest desires. I want you to focus on your top passions, because when you give yourself too many options you can become overwhelmed and pursue them only halfheartedly. Doing this can turn true passions into burnout, because an obligation to do something is not the same as a desire to do something.

## Question 3: How Can You Fit Your Passion into Your Work?

Your answer to this question will bring your work to life, because passion drives consistency, and consistency brings expertise. This is the question you can ask yourself whether you are looking to become an entrepreneur or you find yourself in a nine-to-five job. Wherever you are at with your work, I know you can find something to be passionate about.

Once you discover what it is, exactly, that drives you, you'll be able to focus on it and eventually do it so well that people will want to pay you more for the unique talents you have to offer. You were made to follow your passions, no matter the outcome. Finding your passion is first for you and those around you. Just know that your passion may not look like everyone else's, and that's great.

Von Miller, outside linebacker for the Denver Broncos, is passionate about chicken farming. He studied poultry science in school and now has a small chicken farm in his backyard. His plan after football is to raise chickens full time, but in the meantime, even while he passionately plays football, he is still working in his other passion of chicken farming. Whether your passion is chicken farming or not, there's always a way to fit passion into your work.[12]

If you want to turn your passion into a vocation, finding what you are good at and what the market needs is the only way to be effective with your work. I'm not telling you that passion is enough on its own; you have to put in the work to find success with your endeavors. Financial gain from your efforts will come, but it never comes at the beginning. It always comes after putting in the work.

If you can eventually turn your top passion(s) into a career, then by all means do so. If you find what you are passionate about and are living it out, whether you spend the rest of your life pursuing it as a hobby or you are able to turn it into a career, it will be beneficial to you as an individual and will help you better the lives of others as well. But if you need to stay in the career you're in for the time being, it is imperative that you find passion in it. If the job is less than ideal, you are still impacting people in some way. You can identify your passions and pursue them whatever your job is or wherever in life you are. Life is too short not to.

### Question 4: What Excites You, Gets You out of Bed Early, and Keeps You Up Late? In Other Words, What Do You Find Fun?

This question usually gets lost in the mix somewhere along the way, but this is the kind of motivation that keeps you going even when you don't feel like it. A good sign that you are passionate is losing track of time when you are in your element. You need to pursue what keeps your wheels turning and keeps you curious about life. We need more of our lives to engage us to the point that we leave what we're doing, wanting more.

If you find yourself incurious about life, it is time to reevaluate.

When you challenge yourself and become curious once again, you will find an immediate spark of interest in your life's passions, which in return will make you happier. When you begin doing this, it may not always be easy, but "easy" usually doesn't equate to doing what's important. In fact, very rarely will it be easy to do what's important.

Ask any successful person if their journey was easy, and I can almost guarantee they will tell you there were bumps along the way. But when you find these successful people, also ask them about the mistakes they made along the way. I'm sure they will have many stories to share. Most successful people allow themselves to make mistakes, instead of holding themselves to an unobtainable standard of perfection. Learn to make attempts and have fun along the way.

When you do what excites you, fun will come. Most people forget to have fun, because somewhere along the way, seriousness seems like the only thing to hold on to, but don't buy into that lie. You can do what you love and have fun along the way when you decide that's the way you want to live your life. It is always easier to find passion and, ultimately, bravery when you are having fun. If you can't see fun anywhere around you, go back to a moment of happiness you once had and regain your passion for life.

Along your journey, don't lose sight of why you started in the first place. At some point I hope you were having fun, and if you aren't right now, make it a priority in your life to seek it out again and enjoy what you do. When you love what you do all day long, it's very difficult not to be happy. Who wouldn't want to live a life that can be described as passionate, fun, and happy?

If you stumbled on your journey and you have no idea why you are there, except that it pays the bills, I would recommend questioning why you do what you do. Is it convenient? Is it out of necessity rather than enjoyment? If you were to lose everything and had to start over, would you be doing what you are currently doing? Take the time to dream and ask yourself these questions no matter where you are in the journey. Devote yourself to passion, and the gift of joy that it will give back to you. It is always worth the journey.

### Question 5: What Do You Want to Expound upon in Conversation?

Digital illustrator and storyteller Mars Dorian loves to help people with their businesses in any way that he can. He once gave a stranger at a party advice on building a creative business. This stranger was working a nine-to-five job and wanted to leave it. A few months later, Dorian received an e-mail from this person, thanking him for his advice and explaining how he successfully built his new business based on the ideas Dorian shared with him that night. After this experience, Dorian put more passion than ever into his own business of inspiring others to live and work on their own terms.[13]

Dorian shared his expertise and passion to help a stranger, and you can do the same. What do you love to talk about? What do you go on and on about for hours on end? What topic do you never run out of words for? I'm not just talking about the topics you like discussing; what topics do people look to you for answers on? What do you know a lot about and what are you considered to be an expert on by others? Of course you don't have answers to everything, but on what subjects are you passionate about giving answers?

When people look to you for answers in specific areas, it may signal that you are gifted and passionate about those topics. In other words, the things that you are good at doing usually correlate to what you are passionate about. This is because you have put time, energy, work, and dedication into the things you do well and are now knowledgeable about them.

Another result of working with your passions is creating a healthy confidence within yourself. When you learn to fight your fears, embrace your passions, and discuss how bravery has changed your life, this type of confidence will show up. When you view your passions as part of you, becoming comfortable with them will become second nature.

Answering these five simple questions will help you figure out what you're passionate about. Make sure to write your answers down to these questions, because you will need these answers for a later exercise.

Finding a passion in life is easy, because people are everywhere; it's getting through our fears that can be the difficult part. If not being able to find your passion has kept you stationary, stop making it so difficult. Pick something and move. Stop letting fear keep you complacent, and instead let a passion for life and the world be your driver.

People often get stuck because they think finding passion has to be some big, drawn-out process that takes years, or even an entire lifetime, but that's not true. You can begin pursuing your passion for the world today, but to beat fear, you must step out and pursue your own passion.

Passion can literally change everything. More people don't cultivate passion, because they haven't seen what role it can play in enhancing their happiness and well-being. And the people who treat "passion" as a bad word are those who are unable to find it in their own lives. As twentieth-century poet T. S. Eliot said, "It is obvious that we can no more explain a passion to a person who has never experienced it than we can explain light to the blind."[14] Taste and see just how good passion is. When you do, you won't be able to let it go.

Your passions are too important to ignore. A life without passion is a life without purpose. The passion inside you is there for a reason.

You are wired differently than everyone else, by design. Your passion is there to push you further than you feel like you can go on your own. You were born to find passion and pursue your passions, not only for you, but for something grander than that. Your passion for something greater will help you break through fear and influence people. Know your passions, know your purpose, know what works, and live out bravery.

Peter Sims, founder of Parliament Inc. and author of *Little Bets*, knows this truth all too well. After feeling dissatisfied with his job in venture capital, he started a search in his late twenties for more meaningful work. He discovered his passion to empower people, and helped them unlock their fullest potential—first as an accidental author, and then later as a social innovator and entrepreneur. He followed his curiosity and did his best to listen to his heart.[15]

Like Peter, when you find your unique passion, you will find that it pushes you to dream bigger than ever before. When you think of your own passions and dreams, I sure hope they are huge. So huge, in fact, that they seem impossible to reach. Yes, this means fear is close by, but bravery cannot exist without fear. Never let your belief of things being unobtainable be what stops you. Bravery is meant for the "impossible" and "unobtainable." You are the only person in the world who places limits on your reality. Fight fear and create your destiny.

Passion is a valuable commodity in a world where most people do things without heart. But I want to stress that you can't be halfway interested in your life or your work and make the maximum impact available to you. If you are "sort of" going after something, odds are you won't feel the need to be brave enough. If you aren't filled with passion for the task at hand, you won't live up to it. The journey to bravery requires work, dedication, and immense passion, to push through the fear you will face along the way.

Have you ever caught a glimpse of this passion and experienced the hope that accompanies it? If you have, you know what I am talking about. Living your life with the wonder and amazement that passion brings carries great weight. Hope is found in fighting your biggest fears and finding your passion along the way. I'm all for hope, and I know you are starving for some too. The hope that passion breeds—hope to create a better future for your family, for your business, for your friends, and for the rest of the world—is a beautiful thing. Hope is the beautifully contagious expectation that makes you want to do something grand with your life's passion and to help others find it for themselves too. When you catch wind of passion for a dream and use it to spark hope within yourself, you won't care if the world seems to be working against you, because hope is a much more powerful force.

As I write this, the feeling of hope brings me back to visiting my grandmother, or Nana as I called her, in Selma, Alabama. My sister and I caught fireflies on humid summer nights there too many times to count. I knew that if I could just catch a few fireflies in a jar, they would illuminate the pitch-dark sky and give enough light to last a few more hours. I would run as fast as I could, trying to catch some, and then poke holes in the lid just big enough so they could breathe but small enough so they couldn't escape. I would sit for hours and watch them as their light would shine bright.

I view hope much as I view these firefly experiences. I hoped that I would catch fireflies, not for the act of catching them, but for the bright light they offered. And when I did catch them, I would watch their light in amazement as they brightened the darkness around them. These fireflies didn't realize how much light they were producing, but that is just what they did. When we exude hope with our lives, we do the same exact thing. We bring light to dark and hope to hopeless situations. The world needs to experience doses of hope just like these firefly moments.

The monotony of life can make us forget to see the firefly moments in everything we do and can cause us to lose sight of the beautiful journey we are currently on. This happens when people feel trapped and forget to have fun in the midst of life. Fear settles in among the stress, heartache, pain, and ultimately loss of hope, if we let it. I tell my story of fireflies to remind both you and me about the need for wonder and passion in life. Don't ever lose your firefly curiosity, because that is one of your most precious possessions. This story of fireflies is just one on the drawing board of life that allows me to go back to the source—the force that people need more of is hope.

No matter how hard we try, we will never be able to get away from the need to do great things for the world around us. People need us to reach outside ourselves, to be brave enough to show we care, so we can give away hope freely. Passion and hope are attractive because by embracing them you are saying that to pursue bravery in your life is bigger than fear, and moving forward is the only choice you are compelled to pursue. There's always something more important than fear.

Passion is the answer for all the people who feel stuck in a routine of mediocrity. Passion is the antidote for those who have been giving in to fear for far too long. Passion is what those of you who have lost all wonder and excitement have lost.

Why not live life with more passion? Why not discover more of yourself and become curious about the one wonderful life you have to live? Why not live out your internal drive to influence people with the passion that already resides in you? Without passion, bravery is a matter of luck. When passion is found, bravery becomes a muscle that we can focus on and build into something useful. Life without breathing in passion and exhaling hope is one of wandering aimlessly, trying to find your place in the world. People want and need hope like they need a heartbeat, and people need passion like they need the air they breathe, especially if they are going to make a difference in this world. Once we find these two lifelines, in this passion stage, a commitment to bravery is born.

At points along the journey, while chasing your hopeful opportunities, you don't always have much time to react. In fact, you may be so surprised with opportunities that you will be left with quickly making the choice between standing tall or sitting down and waiting patiently for the next go-round. When you commit to seeing bravery all the way through, passion and hope, paired with good momentum and breakthrough, become much easier to reach. But the good news is that you can begin preparing for bravery right now by finding hope through passion, and when you do, bravery will be waiting.

## Bravery (the End Goal)

In 2002, Markus Zusak began writing *The Book Thief.* He was so passionate about doing the story justice that it took him three years and two hundred different variations to land on his final idea. He wrote it from different perspectives and finally landed on the perspective of death, as we read the story today. When his book was finally released, Zusak said, "In three years, I must have failed over a thousand times, but each failure brought me closer to what I needed to write, and for that, I'm grateful."

Because of the grueling work and perseverance put into the book, it landed on the *New York Times* best-seller list, and stayed there for over 230 weeks. It sold eight million copies, was translated into forty languages, and it wasn't long before the book was turned into a major motion picture. Zusak exemplifies what bravery means to me—it's not giving up and it's also showing up again and again until you succeed.[16]

American novelist Anne Lamott writes, in *Bird by Bird*, "Hope begins in the dark, the stubborn hope that if you just show up and try to do the right thing, the dawn will come. You wait and watch and work: you don't give up."[17]

Bravery is knowing what you need to do and filling the gap between that and where you are currently. This also means that bravery is giving your entire self to repeatedly doing the right things. Bravery isn't a choice that is made once and then you're done with it. You will have to walk this journey at many points in your lifetime, but the good news is that the more you walk it, the easier it becomes. As the saying goes, "When the going gets tough, the tough get going." Toughness finds bravery. The good thing is that bravery is power that is learned, so it can even be found and lived by the weak. It's done by making yourself available and showing up.

The people who have already found bravery weren't born braver than others. They found bravery through their life experiences, by trial and error. Bravery is for you, it's for me, and it's for everyone else out there who has been telling themselves that they need to muster up enough within themselves to face their fears. No matter what fear you are currently facing, there's passion and bravery well within your reach.

There are moments in life when you can see well in advance that you will need a larger supply of bravery, and then there are the moments in life when you will be taken off guard, when shrinking back in fear will look very tempting. It is the moments when you have previously learned to build up bravery and have seen what it can do that will help you find bravery when life catches you by surprise. The more you practice bravery, the more prepared you will be when fear decides to rear its ugly head and you need strength the most.

But before you can accomplish more through bravery practice, you need to have a realistic picture of bravery for yourself. Stop aiming for fearless, because that isn't achievable. All the positive self-talk in the world won't make you fearless. When I see the word "fearless," I can't help but think of all the people who are trying to reach this unobtainable dream. I mean, I see the word everywhere, written in motivational quotes, plastered on the Internet, but I have yet to meet an individual who has been completely fearless. The only time that we can be fearless is in the idea stage, but everything outside that is open to fear. Once we let go of trying to find fearlessness in our everyday lives, we can clear our minds for the most important focus of passion. That's the difference between this book and all the rest—passion is your answer to fighting fear for a lifetime because it is the one thing that helps you to show up time and time again. Overcoming a fear of yours is a one-time fix, whereas passion becomes a way of life that answers the never-ending torment that fear can have if we allow it.

When you know what bravery looks like in your own life, you will know how to act and react with bravery in situations where you used to give in to fear.

The question you need to learn how to answer is this:

## What does bravery look and feel like?

If you've ever wondered what success is, your answer to this question defines it. Nobody can define success for you; only you can do that. This actually reminds me of the time I met a lady who wanted to become a beekeeper. Is becoming a beekeeper my definition of success? Nope. Will leaving her day job to become a beekeeper require bravery? Absolutely. But hearing how passionate she was about becoming a beekeeper tells me that her dreams will eventually win out; it's only a matter of time.

So now, with your top fears and passion in hand, grab your notebook and take as much time as you need to define what bravery looks and feels like to you. If success for you is to become a beekeeper, great! Whatever it is, it's imperative that you define it before we move any further, because this definition is very helpful to focus on at any point you feel your best option is going back to playing it safe.

A friend once told me that "Nothing worth having ever came easy," and it's so true. If it were easy, then everyone would be a rock star in whatever they put their hands to and this whole fear-and-bravery thing wouldn't be an issue. Again, everyone fears, but it's what you do with fear that gets you to bravery. Since we all fear, bravery isn't its absence but rather stepping out in the midst of it with passion in one hand and fight in the other.

A lot of people will tell you to just suck it up and go do something, but without understanding the process of bravery, your mental battle is already lost. The truth is, if you move ahead without knowing that there's a process to bravery, you will end up creating a short-term fix to your fear issues. If you don't go through the process, you miss the importance of passion. And if you don't have passion for what you are pursuing, quitting will be the easiest decision you have ever made. There should always be a reason behind the reason that you do the things you do. When you discover what those reasons are and home in on them, you can fuel the flames of the fire that will keep you moving through fear.

Most people like to think of bravery as this full-blown circus of some sort. A "look at what I did," if you will. But what if I told you that because bravery is built on showing up, it doesn't have to be a huge gesture every time? In a world where busyness stops us from taking opportunities to show up and be brave, and kind, my recommendation for you is to start small and just show up. Start with one thing that will make a difference in someone else's life, and go do it. Why do I recommend this? Once you catch the feeling that showing up gives, you won't be able to stop.

It can be showing up for your daughter's dance recital when you have too much work to do but you know it is the right thing to do. It can be fulfilling a promise to help a friend move. It can be going out of your way to talk to someone different every day, because you realize that there are people out there who need you beyond the few you typically interact with. Bravery can also be learning to say no to less important things so you can tackle your bigger fears and work within your definition of bravery. Again, bravery doesn't have to be grand, but it does take intentionality. It's not always about creating more time in your day, but it is always about being intentional with the time that you already have. In whatever you do, do it with all your might, and with all your passion, so you impact people wherever you go, leaving your imprint on as many lives as possible.

Now, grab your notebook and take ten minutes to write down the names of people you have influenced over the past twelve months and how you specifically showed up in each person's life. No matter how big or how small your brave actions seem, they all count. When you are finished, take the time to reflect and see just how brave you really are. If you're able to identify a lot of people who you influenced with your life over the previous year, then that's an indication of living out bravery. But if you can't think of many people who you have influenced with your life, then that's a good sign that you have withdrawn into a form of fear.

You can use these notes to remind yourself how much you have done over the past year, and to continue to dream about who you want to influence and what you want to accomplish throughout the next twelve months. You should also take time to dissect your fearful moments of not showing up and take away lessons from them too. In retrospect, do you see how you could have applied the bravery process to these moments in some way? How many times did you fear the outcome would be much worse than it actually was? How many times did negative circumstances end up just fine in the end? Hopefully, after you've answered these questions you are left with a positive outlook on your journey. If you have done these exercises and have walked away with a negative outlook on your journey, please know that I didn't ask you to do this for you to reminisce about all your fears. If things in the past didn't turn out exactly how you wanted them to, that's the beautiful thing about the future. Life gives you opportunities to change, to face the road ahead with bravery. And because fear only has the power you hand over to it, you have more control over the road ahead than you may think.

Choosing to stay in fear, and not moving on to find passion and bravery, is a threat because it allows negativity to actively permeate our lives. It's great to get rid of fear and move toward bravery as soon as fearful thoughts and negative emotions appear, rather than dwelling on them because of this fact. But there is more to it than just stopping these thoughts. It takes positive action to fight negative action and find bravery. The longer we hold on to fear, the more we voluntarily allow it to shape our ideals. Fear is then more than a mere thought; it is indeed a terrible way of life.

Taking the notes about yourself you have made in this chapter, it's time to embark on this bravery process together. We need to look at the fears you are facing and what you can do to find bravery in each and every one of them. So if you're ready, we will now look at the root of many of our fears—the fear of inadequacy.

## CHAPTER 2

# The Fear of Inadequacy

Writer and business owner Jenna Arak is familiar with the fear of inadequacy. She has days when she believes she isn't competent enough, productive enough, or talented enough to make what she does a success. Sometimes she feels that the only reasons she has found success are luck and timing. She even says there are days when she feels like an impostor, and that she won't ever quite measure up to the success of other women entrepreneurs. She could easily let her fear of inadequacy be a roadblock, but her passion for what she does has helped her find ways to keep pushing ahead, even when thoughts of inadequacy try to keep her down.[1]

I first found out about Arak when I stumbled across her website and clicked on a link that took me to her essay, "Do I Friend the Dad Who Left?" on salon.com. Her words immediately hooked me: "The first time I saw my father, I searched his face for traces of me, for something that connected us in an indisputable way. I hoped he'd have the same smile or the same long forehead. But I was disappointed to find he was still as much a stranger as he'd been all my life." Of course, I couldn't stop after reading that article and found myself reading through more of her captivating work. I found that in every word she writes there is beauty, and I asked myself, "How can she be dealing with this immense fear? Can't she see how great she is?" Then I realized that Arak isn't alone in her struggle.

Just as Arak has faced her fear of inadequacy and has been able to push through it, I too have faced this same fear many times in my life, and you probably have too. I have experienced the feeling of inadequacy on a personal level, and I hate the paralyzing feelings that accompany it.

Before I made a decision to consciously pursue bravery with all I had within me, I would allow doubt to get in and have its way. Maybe the fear of inadequacy is something you have been dealing with for years, or maybe your entire life, and you are looking for someone, anyone, to understand you and help. But the first step in finding bravery is to admit that the fear of inadequacy is present in your life.

Once you admit that you are experiencing the fear of inadequacy, understanding is on its way. When you understand what your important role is in carrying out your pursuits, you will begin to see what you need to do when first stepping out to tackle your fear of inadequacy. Understand that there is more to this fear than meets the eye. It isn't just the fear you are experiencing that is scaring you. There is more beneath that layer. I know you're exhausted from dealing with the same fear over and over again, but please know that the journey to bravery is contingent on correct movement. And it is only when you bring understanding to your fears and learn how to best deal with them that you will finally be able to move in the right direction.

## The Role of Emotions and Feelings

In 1980 psychologist and researcher Robert Plutchik identified the eight inherent emotions as joy, acceptance, surprise, sadness, disgust, anger, anticipation, and, last but not least, fear.[2] Whatever emotions and insecurities you are having about your current feelings of inadequacy, listening to the signals your body is sending will benefit you and help you better understand the fears you are experiencing. Yes, fear can be a useful thing: it can be a valid indication of circumstances you will face in the future, but can also push you forward, testing you to see if you are truly up for the journey or not.

Kyle Bass, founder and principal of Hayman Capital Management, is one of the brightest minds in the financial business, but the road to get where he is now was anything but easy. It included a few terrible trades, many huge risks, but also many great rewards. Through it all he found ways to look at the fear of inadequacy as a good thing, because it kept him moving in the right direction, even while knowing that fear remained present in his life.

In an interview with Real Vision TV, Bass said that he lives in constant fear. "Again, I live with this constant feeling of inadequacy that drives me so hard to succeed and be a proven fiduciary. . . . And that's what's always driven me."[3] He has been able to change his view on the fear of inadequacy, to see it as a good thing that can propel him forward, and so can you.

Still, the fear of inadequacy does pose some definite dangers, starting with the negative emotions and feelings it triggers, telling us to keep going or to stay away. It is here that you must choose between fears of inadequacy that are merely taking up brain space and the ones that could benefit from more of your attention.

You should first identify the fears of inadequacy that are related to moving toward your passions and jot them down in your notebook. This will help you realize what you care about, regardless of your real or perceived inadequacies. There will be things in life that you just aren't good at, but that's okay. We've still got work to do.

Once you have selected these fears, understand that it is important to identify the tangible skills you already possess and those you have yet to obtain, to help you work through each fear. I recommend developing three of each of those two kinds of skills before tackling your fear of inadequacy. If you have fewer than three, you really should reevaluate. Ask yourself if you are truly passionate about this pursuit and willing to put in the work to pursue bravery. This way you can either stop thinking about it or begin to develop the skills in that area if you are committed to making the journey. If you have more than three skills in each area, it says you have taken the time to develop that particular passion, regardless of your fear of inadequacy.

If you have done this exercise and still have fearful emotions and feel confused as to what approach you should take, you need to ask yourself again if you are committed to what's ahead. Given the present risks, is it worth jumping the hurdles and wrestling with feelings of inadequacy? Is moving forward even a good idea?

It doesn't matter whether you have mastered these areas. What does matter is that you are discovering your passion for life and are working toward becoming brave. You may never become an expert or be "the best," but the fun found in following your passion and fighting fear is often enough to influence the world for good.

Many people say they are passionate about something but haven't spent the time to understand that passion. This tells me that they either don't know where to start or they aren't truly passionate about their pursuit. When we fully understand what it is we are going after and can comprehend the importance of the journey, our negative emotions and resistances will subside.

When we are passionate, we seek to know as much about our pursuit as we possibly can. In the process of doing this, inadequacies—real and imagined—are almost guaranteed to fade away. The key is to become so familiar with your passions and fears that you know every detail about them, because it is this intimate knowledge that will give you the power to help you battle your inadequacies. We fear things most when we don't understand them, and the only way to fight ignorance is to beat our inadequacies by taking action.

It seems like everything in this world is marketed toward making people feel inadequate, from commercials on television to what people post on social media. People are always being made to feel like they need something more, but that's not true. You are already more than enough.

People's wrongly influenced feelings of inadequacy tell them that they aren't good enough to see success, when it is actually fear that is keeping them from ever fully reaching their potential. Yes, emotions can play a huge part in decision making, but giving in to negative emotions is usually giving in too early. If negative emotions are playing a huge part in your decision making right now, I can understand. I have been there. For a long time the fear of inadequacy clouded my vision so I couldn't see how to find bravery in my own life. But when I decided to look at the entirety of the journey I wanted to take and to understand it for what it was, I saw the difference I could make by seeing it through. I was able to catch a glimpse of what was on the other side of fear and to complete the journey through to bravery.

## The Power of Using Your Intuition to Fight Fear

If emotions are what make us human, it is intuition that makes us superhuman. Steve Jobs, former CEO of Apple, said "Intuition is a very powerful thing, more powerful than intellect." He also said, "Have the courage to follow your heart and intuition. They somehow already know what you truly want to become. Everything else is secondary."[4] In the book *Metaphoric Mind*, author Bob Samples refers to theoretical physicist Albert Einstein's belief of the intuitive mind being a sacred gift. He goes on to quote Einstein, saying that the rational mind is a faithful servant, and that it is paradoxical in the context of modern life that we have begun to worship the servant and defile the divine.[5]

Research from University of Leeds shows that our intuition is formed by our previous life experiences and the knowledge we obtain along the way, and it allows us to understand some things almost immediately.[6] People who are able to most effectively use their intuition know who they are, what they are going after, and what they stand for. Using intuition or "following your gut" in areas where you feel inadequacies is a way to live up to your biggest potential, because when we use a balance of intellect (passive smarts), reason (active thinking), and intuition, it is intuition that fills in the gaps. We are wired in such a way that even when all seems lost and there seems to be no way out, if our gut tells us to keep going because we can see a slight chance of success, we will probably continue. You can use this to your advantage in fighting your feelings of inadequacy. But you have to learn to distinguish between intuition and fear.

If the voice of intuition is telling you to quit because you're at a dead end, that isn't inadequacy talking, and you should probably move on to something else. But if it is fear speaking, then give yourself some time. Fear of any kind hates the rational thinking that tells us to keep working while we wait, to grab on to hope, and to keep hanging in long enough to find passion.

When we're in the grip of the fear of inadequacy, we repeat our previous negative experiences, and they become our continuous future reality. This fear halts any forward movement, and keeps us from finding what makes us more than adequate. When this happens, intuition can give us huge doses of momentum. When we let intuition take over instead of our fear of inadequacy, we then have a chance of success.

## Fixing Your Perception of Your "Inadequacies"

None of us wants to feel the anxiety, worry, and unease that the fear of inadequacy causes, but all of us have learned, somewhere along the way, what brings our feelings of inadequacies to the surface and what doesn't. This means that the fear of inadequacy is relative to the individual and to the situations we both encounter and dream up. This also means that the inadequacies we feel can pertain to the past, present, or future, and come in many different forms. So it is important to ask yourself how, exactly, you arrived at the fear of inadequacy you are currently facing. This is because the feelings of inadequacy you are experiencing were very likely picked up along the way, and you need to go back to that moment, face it, and adjust your perception of it.

If you asked me seven years ago what my biggest fear of inadequacy was, I would have told you, without hesitation, that I felt most inadequate when speaking to large groups. Maybe you can relate to the fear that comes with speaking in front of large crowds. If not, you can still apply what I am going to say to the anxiety associated with the main fear(s) of inadequacy you face.

When I would get in front of large groups of people to speak about anything that required expertise, thoughts of inadequacy would run rampant through my head. It was impossible for me to remain focused in those moments, and thoughts would jumble in my head. Words would quickly roll off my tongue, due to fearing silence and dead space. I would get to the end of my talk and want to immediately move on. I apologize to you if you were in the room during those times.

The questions "Am I qualified to speak about this topic?" and "Why am I qualified?" were always present before and after those talks, leading me to doubt my abilities. For me, public speaking became too fraught with self-doubt, because I wasn't listening to the correct voice. But not listening to the right voice wasn't the only reason I felt inadequate. I wasn't taking action. I wasn't practicing and trying to get it right. This only made my feelings of inadequacy worse.

## Practice Makes Perfect (or at Least Adequate!)

The feelings of inadequacy I struggled with largely stemmed from the fact that I was just starting out and didn't have any practice. I was comparing myself to people who already had years of experience with public speaking, and I was confused about why I wasn't there yet. I found, through my own journey, that comparison is a friend to the fear of inadequacy, and practice is its enemy. Be there for others, to encourage them along the way, but never let comparison be your measurement of accomplishment. This is why knowing who you are and pursuing the things you want out of life is so important. When you understand this, you know what makes you different from everyone else, and you will pursue things with confidence in your own strength. In doing this, you become the best you. Until then, you are looking to others for your own definition of bravery.

Practice is the focused action behind what makes you great. The more often you do something, the more confident about it you will become, because you will eventually become more adept at it, no matter how slowly your skills improve. But there's another element to practice that is equally essential to helping you overcome feeling or fearing that you're inadequate: more practice equals more self-belief. Practicing to improve and believing in yourself are the two drivers that will help you stop "aspiring" (to use my least favorite word) and instead become whomever you are longing to be. So whatever your fears of inadequacy entail, practice doing them more often. Although practice may not bring complete perfection, as the popular adage assumes, it will make you far more comfortable with whatever you want to do but are afraid to achieve. Even if you feel inadequate in this moment, you can always practice to become better if you have enough heart behind what you do.

When your fear of inadequacy presents itself, it is mental preparation paired with practice that will make your obstacles diminish and your confidence arise. Think about all the times in school when you prepared for a test and knew every answer on the exam because you prepared—you studied. You felt calm, confident, and comfortable in that moment, right? How about the times you made presentations to your colleagues and knew what you were talking about inside and out? I know you felt empowered and that you could do it over and over again without any issues. Why? Because practice and preparation bring confidence, and confidence moves you toward beating your fear of inadequacy.

Of course there is more to knowing what you are talking about than being willing to practice, but it is the most important ingredient that goes into this recipe. The amount of practice you put in is completely controlled by you, which also means that the amount of work you put in can control how quickly you become better at something, or even how good you become. Many times, the size of return you receive is based on the amount of work that you put into something. When you unlock this powerful key to bravery, you indeed swap inadequacy for bravery and begin fighting your inadequacies more than you ever could without it.

If you are experiencing the fear of inadequacy right now, keep practicing until your fears change through creating braver habits. Phillippa Lally, a health psychology researcher at University College London, found that it takes sixty-six days to create a new habit.[7] You can use this finding to your advantage by concentrating on doing, for those nine weeks, one thing that will move you closer to what you have been seeking. Now, I don't want to overwhelm you, so that's why we are tackling one new habit at a time. Doing this shouldn't be a stress, because it is imperative that it's something you want for yourself. Make it fun! It can be a small move or a big move each day, as long as you show up to become better in the area you want to be more passionate about and grow braver in. Begin to practice this new habit on a daily basis and see just how much fear diminishes in your life.

Patiently putting practice into the right things sets you up for success because it puts good habits into motion, even when fear makes the journey look bleak. If we put practice into the wrong things that we've always done, we will continually get the same results. How many of us repeatedly act out mediocrity expecting to somehow gain success? We keep the routine we have always had, expecting bravery to somehow show up out of nowhere. That's not the way it works. Bravery will only come when you create new brave habits.

When I experienced my own fear of inadequacy about public speaking, I practiced in any way I could to become more comfortable with audiences. I moved out of my comfort zone, had the awesome idea to help others, moved through fear by setting realistic expectations of myself and realizing that comparing myself to others got me nowhere, became very passionate about what I wanted to do and where I wanted to go in life, and found bravery because I knew I could help people with what I had to say. I was put on this earth to help others, and so were you. This is what helped me turn the thing I was most afraid of into the thing I am most excited about. Helping people and sharing ideas is exciting business!

It's funny how the things I used to fear the most were the things I felt most compelled to do, but with writing and speaking I hadn't found passion yet. It had to become bigger than my doing those things just because I could do them. When I admitted I was afraid, it became an internal battle that was up to me to face, more than anything else, and once I found the reason why I needed to follow through, my passion became bigger than fear. As project management software company Basecamp CEO Jason Fried once told me, "If you don't have the internal motivation, you'll likely flare out when the going gets tough." His words couldn't be more true. When your drive or passion doesn't come from within, fear will get in and destroy any momentum you have going.

In my own life, even after becoming comfortable with the topics I speak on, I still continue to practice conveying my message to audiences. I even want to hire a permanent public-speaking coach, so I can become even better at the craft. I never want to be done practicing, and neither should you, because we can always become better at what we do. Even when you are already comfortable with doing what you do, it always pays off to continue practicing, because it is practice that clears out feelings of inadequacy.

As the bravery journey will show you, I didn't somehow skip ahead and jump right into bravery. Let me remind you that nobody gets to do this, and you're kidding yourself if you think you can skip over the parts of the process you don't want to experience. Thinking that you can is like expecting to grow muscles without ever working out. Of course you can wish, if you want, but wanting things to happen without working at them is a waste of time. You won't ever be able to trick fear into becoming a catalyst for bravery without first believing it for yourself. Once you believe, doors will begin to open.

## Tackling New Fears

No, the fear of inadequacy doesn't just go away on its own, but we can learn to handle this fear differently. I mean, I still have fears and so do you. Even when we become comfortable with all our current fears, something else will come our way. However, don't let yourself think that when new fears crop up, you're once again inadequate because you couldn't stay fearless for good. Remember that fear is an important part of life and it will come again. When you realize and accept this, you will learn to move through your fears much more easily than you do right now. And you can always come back to the bravery process and start it again, to tackle every new fear you encounter that tries to block you from achieving your dreams.

My current fear is that no matter what I do or how hard I try, I won't be able to adequately fill every need there is in the lives of others. It's the recovering people-pleaser inside me. There are so many people and so many needs, and I can't possibly have everything that everyone needs, but I am calmed by the fact that I can at least try. (Yes, I can hear Yoda say his famous quote, "Do or do not. There is no try," but that's beside the point.) Finding enough bravery to give life more effort, to try, is key to accomplishing more. To see results, I have, at the very least, to try.

And while being unable to fill everyone's needs is an honest fear, and not necessarily a bad fear to have in moderation, I am also challenged immensely with finding creative ways to influence those around me. It helps to know what is in my control, to work within those boundaries, and to keep pushing the limits.

We all experience the fear of inadequacy at some point in our lives, and a great place to begin is to realize that our struggles and legitimate inadequacies connect us to each other. As *New York Times* bestselling author and thought leader Dr. Brené Brown said, "Imperfections are not inadequacies; they are reminders that we're all in this together."[8] In other words, you can use your fear of inadequacy for good by letting people in. When you share your fears of inadequacy with others, you comfort them by letting them know they're not alone.

Even though all this is true, I know you probably still don't want to hear that the guy writing a book about bravery deals with fears of inadequacy, right? You don't want to hear that I've had issues with speaking in front of large audiences and that I let people down. You probably want me to have huge muscles, tons of tattoos, and carry a sword everywhere I go. I mean, I get it. Pirates are your thing. Well, I'm sorry to break the news to you, but I'm not any of this. Somehow we have gotten a wacky idea of what bravery looks like in our heads, but that's not everyday bravery.

So, what qualifies me to write this book if I still have fears? I will tell you. I have learned how to properly face fear head-on, I have moved into bravery by finding passion for the life that I live, and I have seen this process work every time it's undertaken with care. When you adopt the process for yourself, you will find more self-confidence even in your inadequacies. Self-confidence is about building the drive to do more with your life, not to make yourself look better. If what you accomplish increases belief in yourself by diminishing real or imagined inadequacies, if it raises your spirits and doesn't simply serve the purpose of feeding your ego, then it's a green light to move forward.

In moving ahead with fighting the fear of inadequacy, know that your ego will keep wanting to be fed, but that cannot be the reason for your pursuit. There has to be more to it than that. If I am honest about it, in my lifetime I have done too many things to feed my ego, trying to overcompensate for my feelings of inadequacy. I realized this four years ago when I actually took the time to focus on the different moments when I have successfully fought fear in my lifetime. Yes, the thought of feeding my ego makes me nauseated now, but the only way to respond to it is to evolve as a better me and keep moving. That's the only good response to fear, actually. Keep moving. When you fall, get back up. When you fall again, get back up again. That's your best answer to any mistake, any fear, and any misstep.

Does it feel good in the moment right before you decide to face your biggest fears? Nope. But afterward, you can analyze the fear you were able to fight and then learn from your experience. If you aren't accustomed to it, does it feel good to not receive recognition to enlarge your ego? No. It's not easy when you first change your perspective to one of giving life to others rather than sucking it out of other people and keeping it for yourself. If you aren't already going out of your way and giving up time in your busy schedule to help others, is it easy to begin doing it? Again, no, but if you need more reasons to follow through, I can tell you that doing these things feels great afterward and makes an even bigger impact than you ever could without implementing these principles in your life.

If fighting your fear of inadequacy doesn't come easily to you right now, I promise it will become easier once you take the practices within this chapter to heart. It will mean rewiring the way you think about yourself and the world around you, because that's where we have to learn to fight selfishness and fear at the same time.

Here are the two best questions you can ask yourself when it comes to fighting your fear of inadequacy:

- **How important is it for me to help others?**
- **How important is it for me to move through fear?**

I needed to answer these two questions for myself in order to push through my own biggest fears of inadequacy, and so do you. When you see the value in being able to answer these questions with the words "very important," you will know the reason to finish what you started. When you are able to see this value, you will see the importance of saying yes to more opportunities and following through.

How about instead of focusing on all the flaws you see in yourself, take ten minutes to write down everything you have going for you that makes you more than adequate. Use this time to brag about yourself. I learned from a marriage-counseling session that you can even ask your spouse or a friend to help you with this exercise by pointing out some strengths, even when you can't seem to find them for yourself.

## The Importance of Mentors

One of my fondest memories from the past eight years is sitting down with one of my mentors, Curt. We would meet at the local Panera Bread every week to talk about our marriages, our kids, what we were working on, and life in general. I initially asked him to walk me through a difficult season of life, as I was a new father, and my marriage wasn't doing so well at the time. He had a great marriage and was the father of five wonderful children. I wanted to learn from any advice he could give me, because the life he portrayed had the qualities I wanted in mine. I was there to offer in return anything I could possibly give. It was a very rewarding mentor relationship.

During those morning meetings we would be open and honest about everything, confiding in each other and sharing our biggest dreams. At the time, I was dreaming about what this book might look like, and he was dreaming up different grand ideas for his products. We fed off of each other's creativity, and as a result, we both began trying new things and producing better work. His passion and lack of fear in submitting his ideas to huge corporations encouraged me with fears of my own.

I have found that I am eventually inspired to take action when I go to other people who aren't afraid of something that I feel inadequate about, and let them teach me how they have found success. Do you need to become better at public speaking? Find other people who are great at public speaking and ask them for tips they may have about becoming better at public speaking. I use this example because having mentors has helped me in that area immensely. Their advice played a huge role in helping me overcome my fears, and finding a mentor will only help you with your own fears of inadequacy. But for someone to know that you need help, you must first ask.

Here's a well-known short story that shows just how important it is to get others to help you work through your inadequacies:

A boy and his father were walking through the woods together. They came to a large log that was blocking their path. The boy turned to his father and said, "Do you think I can lift this log, Dad?" The father replied, "If you use all your strength, absolutely you can." The boy rolled up his sleeves, bent his knees, and got his hands under the log. He locked his arms and heaved with every ounce of strength he had, but the log wouldn't budge. He tried over and over again, until at last, exhausted and breathless, he gave up.

He looked at his dad with disappointment and frustration and said, "You told me I could lift it!" His dad smiled and said gently, "I said you could lift it if you used all your strength. You didn't ask me for help." So the boy asked his dad to help him, and together they lifted the log out of their path.[9]

Your strength isn't held by you alone but also by the people who walk alongside you. When you feel unequal to the task in front of you, perhaps it is simply because you aren't using all your strength.

I don't know where I'd be without guidance and encouragement from others. If you ask someone to be your mentor, take the time to gain wisdom from them. From doing this you will also learn how to emulate their actions and gain better results.

Mentors can also be the people who tell you *not* to go in a certain direction. Some people will tell you to ignore the advice of others if you are following your passion, but I can tell you that it's a red flag if people in the industry you are trying to enter tell you that something isn't a good idea. You should at the very least listen to their advice. If there comes a time when industry influencers tell you to use caution, how do you know whether that advice is worth listening to? The key is to know the motive of the person who is offering the advice. Of course a mentor wants you to succeed, but outside of that relationship, knowing if someone is on your side will tell you whether someone should be listened to or not.

And if you needed any more reasons to find a mentor, or to be a mentor yourself, a comprehensive case study conducted by Sun Microsystems from 1996 to 2009 shows that mentors and mentees earn promotions in their careers more often than those who don't seek out mentoring. Mentors are actually promoted six times more often than those who do not mentor formally, and mentees are promoted five times more often than those who are not formally mentored. Also, retention rates are higher both for mentees (72 percent) and mentors (69 percent) than for employees who do not participate in a mentoring program. In fact, their research concludes that the return on investment of mentoring is 1000 percent or greater.[10]

While the responsibility ultimately remains in your hands, mentors will help you get through the fear of inadequacy when you can't seem to push through on your own. Stop living life all alone. Surround yourself with encouragers, and find bravery.

## Find Encouragers to Help You Cultivate Positivity

One of the biggest steps in dreaming up big ideas and beating your feelings of inadequacy is to be courageous enough to allow encouragers in. These don't necessarily need to be mentors, but they are people who uplift rather than tear down. They are the people who always choose to see the best in people, instead of the worst, and you will always know who wants you to succeed by the way they see the good in you before they ever see your flaws. These encouragers can't help you until they know how to, so that's why it is important to learn how to verbalize your dreams.

I remember telling one of my biggest encouragers about my aspirations and his eyes immediately filled with tears. Seeing his reaction made my own eyes fill with tears too. His excitement and passion for my pursuit was contagious. It made me want to go find somebody else to root for, and it also made me want to go put in more work.

I want to be that person for you, to help you through any fear of inadequacy you have, and so do the other encouragers around you. (You can e-mail me at adam@asmithblog.com anytime. I'd love to hear from you.) When you allow encouragers in, you will be able to get over your fear of inadequacy and achieve more with your dreams, because your dreams are meant to be out in the open, not to be held in. It is only when you are open about your dreams that you can allow for others to give you positive feedback. But positivity doesn't begin with getting positive feedback from others; it begins with you. Once you view yourself in a positive light, positivity will flow out of you through your words and actions.

The biggest lie that comes when pursuing a positive outlook on life is that you can't have it now. This lie will tell you that you have to find your positivity in some big success, and on the other side of that you will find happiness, but this isn't true. Happiness can be found now, not on the other side of success, but it has to do with the way you see your life. Even if things aren't going well, it is up to you to change your perception of where you currently are.

Why is this important? Because sometimes the bravest thing you can do is to be happy, when—by anyone else's standards—you should be unhappy. There is something to be thankful for. Part of true success is being happy while doing what you do. I don't know anyone who dreams of success and wants to be unhappy for the entire journey. If you have to show up on a daily basis, you might as well be happy while doing it. If you can practice happiness now, in the present, you will perform better and be more determined to find success.

When you believe that happiness comes only from success, once you fulfill one ideal of success, you will come up with another that you think will make you happier in the future. With this mentality, nothing will ever be good enough to satisfy your happiness craving. Instead, you can be happy now, by living in a constant state of positivity instead of a constant state of negativity.

Seeing the positivity in life is *not* the same as blindly refusing to see the negative things happening around you, as some people like to claim. It is important to take a realistic approach, but that doesn't prevent you from making your approach positive as well. With positivity, you can decide ahead of time that when fear comes you will see it as a lesson, rather than a dead end. It is your outlook on life that determines what you do when life doesn't go exactly as planned.

If you want something to change, the choice begins with you. Give yourself permission to apply positivity to every area of your life and watch what this alone can do for you. A happy and positive individual, family, and team is always more productive than a negative one. Think about this: Which drives a better relationship, a negative trait such as fear or a positive trait such as love? It is always the positive trait, love. Fear disrupts communication, while love allows for more expressive communication to take place. You will always want to do more for the people you love rather than for the people you fear, and you will want to be with those people more often as well. You can have that same effect on others when you possess positivity in your own life.

Once you experience what positivity feels like, you will want to stay there. The issue is that people have become far too comfortable living in a constant state of negativity. However, we can push through negativity when we fully understand just how much power it can and will have in our lives if we allow it to. The best way to know if you have been putting positivity or negativity into your life is to look at your thoughts, emotions, and reactions. Your thoughts will tell you a lot. Are they negative or uplifting? Are your thoughts full of bravery or fear? When you have a positive outlook on life, you will tend to think about the good in things. Since positivity starts with you, let your thoughts be positive and filled with life. Do this and let your mind be free to enjoy life to the fullest. Life is too short to let negativity take over.

Are you down in the dumps on most days, feeling depressed, sad about the circumstances of your life? Or are you full of joy and positivity? Don't let negative emotions dictate where your day will go. Take over your emotions and use them to help guide you. Never let them be your master. Yes, we were made as emotional beings, but it's up to us to respond to our emotions and use them to our advantage, to let them tell us if we are leaning toward positivity or negativity.

Take a look at your reactions to everyday moments. Is your tendency to fly off the handle at any little thing, or do you take most situations in stride? How you react says a lot about which way you lean and what you have been putting into life. Anger comes out when negativity has been poured in, and peace and calmness come out when you focus on positivity. Focus on bringing a calm to the storm and see just how good life really is.

I am reminded of a quote from bestselling author and entrepreneur Chris Guillebeau, who understands the importance of having positivity in one's life. In the June 2010 issue of *Fear.less Magazine*, he said:

In the writing and entrepreneur world, I have many fears—fears of judgment, of being misunderstood, of being marginalized, of letting other people down. Each of these can be paralyzing forces if you let them consume you. What I've found really helps me is positive reinforcement. I keep a file of nice things people have said and that file only exists for me—it's only there for when I want to look at it, and I don't look through it that often, but it's nice to know it's there. Even though it's true that negative feedback is more damaging than positive feedback is affirming, as you begin to receive positive feedback, pay attention to it. It helps to ground yourself and get a sense of perspective around the negative feedback you receive.[11]

Even if allowing others in increases the possibility that negativity can be spoken into your life, I love that Guillebeau understands the need for paying attention to the positivity that comes our way. Positivity is an amazing gift that you can give to others and receive for yourself as well.

Do you want more positivity in your life? Your answer is to put more good into it. Read healthier books, surround yourself with more uplifting and courageous people, and speak life into others. That is how you control your outlook on life. The more belief you can pour into yourself from outside influences, the more you will believe in yourself. If your past has been full of negativity, and it's difficult to find hope even in your present situation, know that it is never too late for things to change for the better. Positivity tells you that you are more than adequate: You are brave.

## Letting Go of the Past and Mediocrity

If it is your past that is holding you back in the fear of inadequacy, and you are afraid to step out because of something that happened years ago, you cannot allow that which is already done and gone to hold you back indefinitely. Your past is what has prepared you for today. If you are worried about what the future holds and that is what keeps you from tackling your inadequacies, then don't let your fear of the future hold you back either. The past chains us to our inadequacies, but when we look to the future and see potential there, we claim the possibility of greatness that is ahead of us.

When you allow past, present, or possible future outcomes to bring the fear of inadequacy into your life, you retreat into safe, mediocre routines and lull yourself to sleep. It isn't always a quick jolt that knocks us off course. It's often a slight veering off course over a long period of time. Frequently we don't even notice when we first go off course, and end up continuing down the same wrong path. When you get to this point in life, you have become content with what life decides to bring you, instead of putting in the work and beating your fears of inadequacy. You either settle in, comfortable enough, and take what you get, or you push forward to create what you get and leave safety behind. When you do the latter, you are well on your way to finding bravery.

If you don't learn to leave safety behind, you will never discover the meaning of life, missing all the beauty that life has to offer. If you are still hesitating, stop being okay with becoming the person you don't really want to be. Maybe you feel that you have only been coasting for a little while, but remember that while the complacency that allows the fear of inadequacy to take over doesn't strike overnight, it quietly grows until the next correct step is unclear.

Complacency creeps in, along with the fear of inadequacy, to steal your life away subtly, so much so that you don't even notice what's happening. Some people wake from their slumber twenty years later and wonder where all the time went and wish they had done a better job living out bravery. The good news is that this doesn't have to be you. You don't have to settle for the fear of inadequacy and the mediocrity it inevitably brings. No, fighting the fear of inadequacy isn't comfortable, but it allows you to find the very best you.

Once you fall for the lies that are haunting you and believe that you are inadequate, the easiest thing to do is settle for just getting by, while bravery requires a lot more than that. Mediocrity consists of believing that you are inadequate and not pursuing life for all it has to offer, stumbling on good things every once in a while without any intention, plan, or passion. This will become the habit you will live out once you give in to these lies. Don't give in to the temptation to play it safe. Instead, begin using your fear of inadequacy to create bravery momentum right now.

## Dream Big and Apply the Bravery Process to Tackle Inadequacy

When you live out your passion, you will see bravery begin to transform your fear of inadequacy. It's only a matter of time. When you put enough passion behind something, you are unstoppable. I knew my own passion was to help people achieve their wildest dreams, so I began a life-coaching and consulting business along with owning another business, began writing more, and speaking. Among the people I spend time with and coach, I find over and over that the biggest obstacle we face in our lives is fear. And if we keep retreating every time it appears, we will never reach our full potential in life.

When I first started taking people through my coaching program, my fear of inadequacy sounded something like "Who are you to tell people how they should live?" The answer that came to me was that my journey qualified me to do so, and your life experiences qualify you to impact others too. Before I began working with passion, I was exhausted with not living a brave and intentional life. I had stayed with a job for longer than I should have, I wasn't valuing my family enough, I wasn't focusing on my love of helping people, and I was coasting through life unaware of the importance of every single moment.

After hitting my head against the wall enough times, I began to focus on what was truly important. I knew I had to accomplish more, and maybe that's where you are today. Maybe after all these years of getting nowhere and not becoming the person you want to become, you are finally ready to set out on your own journey and find the bravery to work through your fears of inadequacy.

Do you have huge dreams you currently feel too inadequate to unleash and discover? Are you afraid to tell others about them because you prefer to stay safely undiscovered in your nine-to-five job? (Not that there's anything wrong with a nine-to-five job.) Are you satisfied with just creating on the side? Maybe you do feel safe and okay about not being a risk-taking artist or well-known speaker or *New York Times* bestselling author or a top-rated chef or incredibly lauded soccer player or a social worker who saves lives or a full-time student who gets the education he or she has always desired? I know that once I told other people about my biggest fears and who I truly wanted to become, I felt accountable. That one small action made me feel even more compelled to face my fears. This may be uncomfortable, but when dealing with your fears of inadequacy, sometimes this is just the push you need.

Maybe your fear of inadequacy has you so discombobulated that you don't know where to begin. Maybe you have put your dreams on hold because you fear inadequacy and have found comfort in taking a backseat rather than sitting in the driver's seat and taking the wheel. Maybe you have put things off and are hoping that one day your biggest dreams will somehow find you. But life doesn't ever happen this way. You won't find bravery by merely thinking about the process. Life happens the way you make it happen through your actions. The bravery process always requires movement.

When the fear of inadequacy creeps in, you may think that the only option is to stay still, in the moment, but that's a lie. You have tricked yourself into thinking within too many boundaries and have refused to give yourself moments to dream with reckless abandon. Allow yourself to be free when dreaming—don't hold back. Your dreaming deserves openness, the vulnerability to discover what is really inside you. When you dream big, you allow yourself to be free from the chains of fear that are trying to hold you back. There is no way you can be inadequate when you dream big and accomplish what you set out to do.

Your dreams are meant to be so big, in fact, that you think they sound strange when you tell people about them. They are the dreams that you are tempted to stuff down so deep inside you that nobody can ever know about them. They are the same ones that are too personal and too dangerous to let people know about. If people knew about them, they might think differently of you, but you need to come to terms with this. Your uniqueness is what makes you amazing. When you let these dreams out, you quit letting silence empower your fears of inadequacy and will instead see that you are already more than enough. Affecting the world has to become more important to you than what a few others think of your ideas. Let your passion and huge dreams guide you, rather than letting your fear of inadequacy stop you.

If you have contemplated giving up on your dreams because of your fears of inadequacy, you should go back to a moment when you knew who you were and find healing in that. Go back before the world told you what you needed to be or what you needed to do, before you made a mistake and let your past dictate your future. Go back to before you believed in a negative self-perception, before you allowed inadequacy to be set as your personal identity.

Remind yourself of the reasons you are where you are today, and start over if you need to. It's fine to start over, but it isn't okay to stand on the sidelines, hoping that your inadequacies will somehow disappear and your dreams will somehow happen on their own. Step out with bravery, and believe you are more than capable of achieving your dreams once and for all, even when you are uncertain of what your future holds.

## CHAPTER 3

# The Fear of Uncertainty

Why didn't Kodak, the camera giant, start Instagram? It's called the fear of uncertainty. Film was a huge industry in 1992, and digital cameras were still a very new idea. Kodak at that time was busy focusing on their passion for 35 mm film cameras and processing. Their success was based on an ingenious business model. They sold film, they sold the chemicals used to develop film, and they sold the paper that photographs were printed on. They were unstoppable, or so they thought. They refused to change with the times and eventually lost their way. They became complacent, went through a restructuring, and are now in the process of trying to find their core business identity and mission once again.

The other big company of the film era that didn't start Instagram was Polaroid. When Gary T. DiCamillo, a former chief executive at Polaroid, was interviewed on the company's problems, he knew what their biggest issue was. He said, "We knew we needed to change the fan belt, but we couldn't stop the engine. And the reason we couldn't stop the engine was that instant film was the core of the financial model of this company. It drove all the economics."[1]

Both Kodak and Polaroid started out well—even bravely, you might say. But over time, they failed to adapt to the changing marketplace. Rather than returning to the all-important idea phase of the process, they got stuck in the complacency and fear stages.

What were they so afraid of? The fear of uncertainty, of not knowing what the future holds and being too afraid to find out, lest they didn't like what they discovered. Instead of embracing digital developments and innovations as new channels for growth, asking the right questions to understand where the digital age was moving their industry, and learning how these developments were changing their customers' needs so they could better serve them, these companies became frightened by this unknown new world and decided to stick with what they were familiar with. As a result, they missed out on huge opportunities and were left struggling to catch up in the wake of the digital revolution.

If you don't want to be like Kodak and Polaroid, you're probably wondering, "Adam, how do you begin to ask the right questions?" Let me share a really effective six-step technique a friend of mine taught me that I have used ever since.

- First, you should shift your perspective. Think about the following: What concerns do your customers have? Your boss? Your peers? Your friends? Your family?
- Second, you should test different time scales. Near term, longer term. What new problems will arise later? Once you make a decision and begin to act, what forces will you encounter?

- Third, put on your project-manager hat. Ask about scope, duration, resource needs, and the necessary level of focus.
- Fourth, review all your options. Compared to what? What else might be considered? What assumptions were made?
- Fifth, check the emotions involved. Ask how people feel about it—scary good or scary bad? It's not enough to get the facts—you should test emotional content.
- And, sixth, use the "WW___A" (What would ____ ask?) strategy. Pay attention to what other successful people ask, and how they ask. Become a student of other successful people. Some people are so good at asking questions that they no longer are conscious of why they're asking. Observe, and when they ask a particularly good question, ask them why they asked it.

These questions would have been perfect for Kodak and Polaroid to ask. If they had, they might have seen the opportunity they were missing out on. Fast-forward twenty-five years, and the digital age is booming. Most teenagers don't even know how to operate a film camera, but they definitely know how to use their smartphones.

So instead of a big corporation starting Instagram, thirteen individuals were able to see the need for a social media photo-sharing app, and capitalized on the complacency of Kodak and Polaroid. They were able to do what many people do not—fight the fear of uncertainty. They saw the potential in building the company's worth over time, and didn't succumb to the need for instant gratification. Instagram wasn't earning money in the beginning, but its future earning potential was off the charts. As they did, know that you may sometimes need to sacrifice in the beginning to get to something better in the future. Facebook saw the potential of Instagram and purchased it in April 2012 for a cool billion dollars. People are passionate about social media, and Instagram has been growing ever since.

But you want to know what would have saved Kodak and Polaroid even more heartache? Well, actually two things—anticipation and vision. Anticipating what will happen in the future is a strength that can be developed, and it will help you take the first step when you experience the fear of uncertainty. And vision is what will keep you moving forward regardless of your fears. In whatever you do, anticipation and vision are both necessary ingredients to fight the fear of uncertainty.

## Anticipation

We've already discussed intuition, which is a gut feeling that typically comes into play when one is already in a situation. That's good, but what about when you need to be able to foresee potential opportunities or problems *before* you get into a situation, so you can take advantage of them or sidestep them? That is anticipation, and it plays a key role in helping people diminish their fears of uncertainty. Developing good anticipation skills means paying more attention both to your intuition and, more important, to what's happening around you, so you can anticipate opportunities and seize them or predict potential problems and avoid or resolve them before they become big issues. To put it more succinctly, if we wait to listen to our intuition, chances are that we are already experiencing our fears. When we take time to anticipate, we are preparing the way for success by taking precautions, to get things right.

In my own life, in my writing, and in business, the number one thing that has made me successful is anticipating the needs of others.

If you can give people what they need before they actually need it, you will begin to build trust, and those people will keep coming back for more. You would probably think that I found the importance of anticipation in my own business, but I originally learned about anticipation from the staff at the Ritz-Carlton in Atlanta, Georgia.

One year for Valentine's Day, I landed on the idea of taking my wife, Jasmine, to the Atlanta Grill, on the first floor of that stunning hotel. When I called to make reservations, I could already tell that the caliber of service was different. After I scheduled our dinner, the receptionist followed with one last question: "Adam, can I have wine and flowers at your table for you and Jasmine when you arrive?" I had already taken care of those items, but it was the thought that left an impression on me. Not only did she want to know both of our names, but in all our years of eating out on Valentine's Day, no one had been so thoughtful as to ask me such an anticipatory question. She saw our possible needs before we asked for anything, and it made an impact that we still remember to this day.

When we arrived at the restaurant, the valet took our car, and we headed inside. Someone was there to open our door as we walked into the building, and just like the lady on the telephone, he already knew our names. When we walked into the restaurant, the lady who seated us knew our names, as well. This was no coincidence: they had anticipated our arrival. As she sat us at our table, she put our menus down and placed napkins in each of our laps. She also covered our glasses with her hand as she poured water, just in case any were to splash in our direction.

The rest of the evening's service was just as remarkable, and I learned something valuable from the service I experienced that night: you will make a bigger difference in the world by anticipating the needs of others. The reason I remember that specific Valentine's Day is not the food we ate (it included caviar and I don't have a fancy palate) but the way those individuals treated us. And the good news is that leaving a positive impression isn't difficult to do; all you need to do is increase your awareness and anticipate the needs of others more often. It's that simple, and it's never a waste of time.

No, you will not get to the end of your life and think, "I just did too much good with my life. I wish I had cared less about others." In fact, it might be quite the opposite. The fearful question you may ask in the end could sound something like "Did I do enough?" More often than not, this is the question people ask themselves in their final hours, but it doesn't have to be this way. Being proactive and anticipatory right now will keep this fear of uncertainty from creeping up in the future. You can get to the end of your life and be satisfied with what you did by being aware and anticipating.

So how can we become better at exercising anticipation? Begin by caring more about the experience that people encounter when they come in contact with you and/or your business. The second step is to be more patient in decision making to ensure that immediate needs aren't the only needs being addressed. Of course, to anticipate you must be able to make educated predictions about the future. Making decisions in a hurry can cause excitement to cloud one's perspective. When you learn how to cut through the excitement that making decisions brings, you can focus on the real issues at hand. You can do this by anticipating all possible outcomes first, and then once the outcomes have been decided, you can scale your conclusions back to reality. Here it is important to combine a firm grasp of reality with an open mind for possibilities. Begin with thinking broader, and then get rid of the excess to find your best possible answer in anticipating the needs of others. "What is the worst that can happen?" is a great question to ask yourself in these times.

Stop dreaming up false fears beforehand, and instead begin being more realistic. Fighting your fears requires you to be realistically proactive, not reactive. Being proactive leaves less room for error, making you more confident and asking better questions in the end. If Kodak or Polaroid had anticipated the success of digital media, they wouldn't be in the reactive state they are now.

Once you come up with the best solution, it is time to take action. From my experiences, I have learned that I need to anticipate so I can take the best possible action in the future. Of course, you will know whether you get it right or wrong by comparing your anticipations and outcomes, but the fact that you are looking ahead says you are headed toward bravery.

## Look at the Facts

When the fear of uncertainty is present, it is usually because things are being blown out of proportion before they even begin. Maybe you even took the time to make calculated anticipations, but your anticipations were still off. And now you have forgotten to look at your present factual reality. Sure, you can spin what research says to uphold your beliefs, but that's not truth—that's opinion. Opinions consist of spinning the truth someone wants to listen to in an attempt to solidify one's belief. But forget about your current opinion for a moment. What is really happening? Stop focusing on being an optimist or a pessimist—it's time to be a realist.

We discussed emotions previously, but facts are even more important, because facts cannot lie. In former United States president John Adams's "Speech in Defence of the Soldiers," he said, "Facts are stubborn things; and whatever may be our wishes, our inclinations, or the dictates of our passions, they cannot alter the state of facts and evidence." The more we can focus on things until they become as clear as simple addition, the better.

This is also how we need to approach the fears in our life. When fears look too big to overcome, we should ask, "What are the hard facts?" This requires us to anticipate the problems that may arise and to begin looking at the facts as black and white, instead of overwhelming gray areas. Of course, life does include many gray areas, but the more often we can decide on the answers beforehand, the less fear will enter our actions and reactions.

If the facts tell you that your fear of uncertainty is unwarranted, then it's probably time to take the first step. But if the facts tell you that you should be uncertain, it's time to reevaluate the situation. Is it worth taking the next step? Is there a way to make things more certain? Is your fear validated in the facts? If your answers to these questions are the answers that you wanted to hear, then by all means keep pressing forward with passion. But if the facts are not telling you good things, then it is your responsibility to either change your idea or grab hold of a new perspective, with a vision for the future.

## Create a Vision

One of my good friends, Chris, went through boot camp about ten years ago. I never thought he would go into the military, but both his dad and grandfather were in the air force, so in a way it made sense that he would follow in their footsteps. I talked to him on the phone one day after he made it through boot camp, and he told me it was difficult, but he didn't seem to convey just how difficult I knew it had to be. After our discussion, my realization was that his passion and fight for bravery had everything to do with the vision he had for his life. He understood that boot camp was just another part of the journey he needed take to join the air force.

His goal was to become an air-traffic controller for the air force, develop the proper skills, and move on to become an air-traffic controller for the FAA. These steps would give him the skills needed to excel with his job in the future, and he was willing to fight his fear of uncertainty to find success with his endeavors.

Although it was very hard for him to endure two months of boot camp—waking up early every day, running crazy long distances, being away from family, having his food knocked on the ground by a training instructor, and having other instructors yell at him—his passion and vision far outweighed the temporary struggle he had to endure. He had a vision of who he wanted to become, and his fears weren't going to stand in his way. He did eventually leave his position as an air-traffic controller with the air force to take his dream job as an air-traffic controller for the FAA. He had a vision for his life, found passion in his work, made a plan, and then patiently worked the plan until he reached his goal.

Having a vision for your life and a plan for what you want to do with it is imperative to fight fear, but far too often people don't identify what they want to do with their life, which leaves them playing it safe. What they don't understand is that it is much easier to end up at a destination when you have it marked on a map. How well has it worked for you to wander aimlessly, hoping you will somehow arrive at your destination? If this is how you navigate, remind me to never take a road trip with you.

When people tell me they don't have a plan for their life, my next question is always, "When is the last time you were brave enough to dream?" Planning requires dreaming. I would dare you to dream a five-year plan and picture yourself at a different spot than you are in today. If your plan doesn't have you growing in some way in the next five years, that's fear talking, and you need to come up with a different plan. But if you are willing to dream and take risks, you are well on your way to creating a worthy plan for your life. All you need is a little imagination.

When you look at your dreams, do they make you want to take action? I ask you this question because big goals that are written down make individuals 90 percent more productive than individuals who do not have compelling goals.[2] If you read over your dreams and don't feel motivation sparked within you, it's time to reword them. You need passion to spark determination, so action can take place. Take the time to word the vision you have for your life so well that it makes you want to get up and go after your ideas. If your dreams don't motivate you, they won't motivate anyone else. If this is where you currently are with your dreams, you may need to look at creating new a vision for your life, or coming up with new dreams altogether.

When you create enticing ideas and pursue them, passion will drive you to places you have never gone before. Finding passion even decreases your uncertainty, handing you back more control over your life in newfound territory. There's no stopping you when you choose to clutch passion tight as you pursue your ideas. It's actually the only way to create consistent luck for yourself.

You can begin creating a better vision for your life by taking the ideas that you have written in your notebook from earlier and plugging them into the SMART goals concept, which has become a popular method for businesses, organizations, and individuals around the world to determine what ideas they want to pursue to achieve the success they seek. (Some individuals and businesses use the OKR method—objectives and key results method—but I have always used the SMART method, so that's what I'm comfortable with. Use what works for you.) As you may or may not know, SMART stands for "specific, measurable, achievable, relevant, and time-bound" goals. All your ideas should fit this description, which will help you to see what you need to do on a daily, weekly, monthly, and yearly basis to achieve your detailed goals. Captivating ideas give vision and purpose to your life, and will help you get through the adversity you will face along the way. In other words, vision is where you see yourself in the future, and following through on your daily, weekly, and monthly ideas is what will get you there.

Now, I want you to take this one step further. Once you have your SMART ideas, I want you to draw a three-column idea chart in your notebook, which includes your ideas, your fears, and your passions (all of which you wrote down previously) so you can easily see how all three areas correlate. Again, your SMART goals are what you truly want from life, your fears are the things that are standing between you and success with your ideas, and your passions are the things that are propelling you forward. The chart should look something like this:

| IDEAS | FEARS | PASSIONS |
|-------|-------|----------|
|       |       |          |
|       |       |          |
|       |       |          |

Doing this exercise will tell you if your fears are greater than your passion, or your passions greater than the fears you are facing with your ideas. Your answers will tell you what your next step should be.

And if your answers aren't what you want to see, then you always have the power to make the necessary changes to turn things around for the better.

Identifying your SMART ideas will increase your chances of making it through to bravery, even when you don't necessarily feel like going through the process. This is because the clearer you are with the vision you have for your life, the more informed you are of the next steps you need to take, and the better your odds are of finding success. When you stick to the plan and see your ideas as your primary source of encouragement and determination, you will learn to show up where your plan tells you to. Of course, plans aren't perfect, and many things happen in life that you can't plan for, but the main benefit of having a plan for your life is that it brings a small level of certainty in what would otherwise be uncertain.

Uncertainty is the one thing that will compel you to shy away before you get to see your own potential, but you don't have to listen to the lies that your fear of uncertainty brings. When there is passion behind your pursuit, you will find bravery and will be able to commit, even when faced with uncertainty. But remember that part of finding your unique passion for life and being smart about the ideas you pursue is to find what you are good at. Your strengths are there to help you fight your fears and reach the vision you have for your life.

## Know Your Strengths and Take Smarter Risks

According to research done by Gallup, people who are committed to using their strengths every day are six times more likely to be engaged on the job.[3] That exciting news means more bravery and less fear in the workplace. This tells me that you should know your strengths and develop them relentlessly. I know my biggest strength: I'm great at building relationships. And I've built businesses that keep me continually building relationships with people. I know my strengths, and I am always trying to find the best ways to implement them every single day.

When we develop ourselves in one specific field and become great in it, taking risks within that area becomes a no-brainer. Yes, I am all for risks, but calculated risks are the only risks worth taking. An example of someone who understands the importance of this is the Environmental Protection Agency's chief information officer, Ann Dunkin. She left the private sector more than six years ago, and in every job she has had, her goal has been to communicate to her employees the importance of taking smart risks. In an interview with *Nextgov*, Dunkin said, "We tell them [our employees], 'We don't want you to take stupid risks; we want you to take smart, carefully thought-out risks.'"[4]

I've applied this rule of taking smarter risks in every venture I have pursued, and it has worked well for me. Plain and simple: taking smarter risks is decision making at its best. The Elon Musks of the world want to fly rockets to the moon, but that's just not a smart risk for me to take. Yes, we need people like Musk to continually push the envelope, but I don't have Elon Musk–type money. And in case you don't know who Elon Musk is, he's the CEO and CTO of SpaceX, CEO and product architect of Tesla Motors, chairman of SolarCity, cofounder of PayPal, and cochairman of OpenAI. Now, if you want to go into the rocket business, I won't be the one to stop you, as long as your drive isn't a selfish ego trip. Remember, people first, and I guess flying people to the moon could help them in some way. Keeping people at the center of business is the only good reason to be in business, and improving quality of life for others is the only reason that I do what I do.

My motto for harnessing my entrepreneurial spirit has always been, "Build a business that everyone needs and that makes them happy." This motto was important when I started my life-coaching business and when I invested in a footwear company. People need guidance, and people need shoes. I'm just here to help and to bring positivity wherever I go.

Smart risks in business include a large potential client base, and combining that with the ability to charge a premium never hurts. If you have a lower potential client base, of course you need to charge even more. Profits depend on overhead in either scenario, but the key is to fill an actual need. This of course creates less potential risk. Smart risks apply to business, but they apply to your personal life as well. Be smart when you take a jump. Don't rush into things, and keep a level head. That's good advice no matter who you are.

I have had plenty of uncertainty in my life, as you probably have too. But whenever I felt motivated enough to test the waters, I eventually found what I was looking for. Passion is the antidote for your fear of uncertainty, because it gives you something to hold on to as you take smarter risks. For every risk you take there is a lesson or reward found in bravery. And if you are wondering whether you should take a particular risk, just know that not taking a risk is often the riskiest thing you could do.

## When You Aren't Willing to Do the Work

Today, Disney rakes in billions of dollars from merchandise, movies, and theme parks around the world, but Walt Disney himself had a rough start with work. He was fired by a newspaper editor because "he lacked imagination and had no good ideas." After that, Disney started a number of businesses that didn't last very long, and the repeated flops left him with a fear of uncertainty. He kept putting the work in, however, and eventually found a recipe for success. He understood that taking risks, persistence, and hard work always pay off, especially when adversity comes.[5] Unfortunately, many people don't look at life in the same way Disney did.

Unlike Disney, many people try to find ways to work much less, but this just moves us, and our society, far away from one of the most important reasons we were all created. Putting our hands to tasks, using our brainpower, and working alongside others are all beautiful aspects of becoming brave in our work, and it's our responsibility to learn how to best fight the fear of uncertainty with these tools in our arsenal. It is only when we put in the necessary work that we will create something beautiful with our lives.

It took me ten years of maintaining personal blogs, social media posts, and articles to actually make the time to sit down and write a book. In the beginning, I wasn't fully committed to putting in the hard work that it takes to write a book, and I used excuses more often than not. But as I became more passionate about writing, my fears subsided, and I found bravery instead.

Don't bother looking for shortcuts through your fears of uncertainty, because there aren't any. If you fear uncertainty, it's probably because you haven't put the work in yet. Put the work in and reap the reward. That is the best, most honest advice I could ever give you. I care too much about you to tell you otherwise.

## Taking Action in Uncertainty

One rainy night, as my family and I were driving home, we heard a horrible car wreck happen directly to the left of us. I saw it out of the corner of my eye and knew it had to be bad. We pulled over in a nearby gas-station parking lot so we could assist with the situation, because obviously these people needed help. We could see that two cars were involved in the accident, but all other details were unknown at that time.

As I began moving quickly toward the accident, trying not to get hit by oncoming traffic, a female driver came running toward me asking, "What do I do? What do I do? What do I do?" in a very panicked voice. The only response I could come up with was, "You have to remain calm," followed by, "Has someone dialed 911?" She replied, "Yes, the man over there is dialing 911." I quickly asked, "Do you need to call anyone?" She did, so I gave her my phone to make the calls she needed to. As she was dialing her dad, she hysterically said, "The man, the man in the other car . . . he was ejected . . . the car is on top of him. What do I do?" I thought, "What?!" and then quickly made my way over to the scene of the crash. It was horrific.

The cars had spun around and were facing completely different directions. Glass from their windows littered the streets, and bumpers were lying there as if they'd been plucked off like twigs. Human life is fragile, but until that moment I had never quite seen, up close, how fragile it could be.

It looked as if the female's car had slid on the slick roads and T-boned the male driver's car, which then forced him to slide and hit a concrete pole head-on. Concrete poles don't budge, but cars sure do. The impact from the crash ejected him out of his car, and left him lying facedown on the sidewalk, with his car on top of him, pinning his limp body to this solid concrete pole. I am not built for this kind of bloody work, and I sure do respect paramedics who have the stomachs for it. As I stood there, paralyzed by what I saw, I felt like crying and vomiting all at the same time, but I somehow held my composure together.

At first we debated whether it was best to get the car off him or if moving the car would hurt him more. My first instinct was to get the car off him, because I thought it would provide some relief, but somewhere along the way I remembered hearing that you shouldn't move a person who was severely injured, so I was uncertain about what to do.

About a minute later, a man ran up to us screaming, "Get the car off him!" He sounded pretty sure that we should move the car, so we did, and I'm glad we followed his advice. The paramedics showed up about two minutes later, and they were able to quickly rush the injured man to the emergency room since the car had already been lifted off him.

Surprisingly, the man who was pinned underneath his car survived, but the whole situation made me realize what uncertainty can do. When I arrived on the scene, I had no idea what I should do or how I could help. Uncertainty can dictate outcomes, for better or for worse.

In this scenario, my actions were extremely important, but in other situations my words were more important to the outcome. In the past, there have been times when my words haven't matched up with what I was doing. What I was saying might have sounded brave, but the uncertainty shown in my actions definitely didn't reflect bravery. In these moments, fear would arise and immobilize me so I didn't know which way to go or what to do next. I mistakenly decided that opportunities would have to find me if they wanted to happen, when I should have been going and finding them. The state of inaction is the very worst place to find ourselves, but uncertainty loves making us stall out. It's during these times that we begin to question our own abilities, and many times people can talk themselves out of moving forward because they've allowed their uncertainty to grow too large.

In fact, one of the biggest problems in this world is that people don't follow through on their original intentions with action. Good intentions are great and all, but it takes more than good intentions to make things happen. Results require action. Without action, lives don't change. The truth is that fear diminishes when we are familiar with what is happening, and the only way to become more familiar with the uncertain is to take a first step.

The fear of uncertainty has shown up many times in my life, leaving me to think about all the possible outcomes. This fear was founded in not being able to fully see the results of my actions beforehand. In these moments I experienced fear in proportion to my ignorance.

Maybe for you it's taking the next step within your career or finally sitting down long enough to put words on a page to start forming your new book, or maybe it's finally sitting down to have that much-needed conversation with a friend, or even a current foe, or maybe you simply need to finish what you began. Whatever it may be, know that you already have enough within you to accomplish your wildest dreams. You are worthy of certainty. You are enough.

## CHAPTER 4

# The Fear of Failure

One of my favorite movies is *You've Got Mail*, starring Meg Ryan and Tom Hanks. The title of the movie comes from the way America Online's mail system says, "You've got mail" when new e-mail arrives in your in-box. If you can remember that, then you can remember dial-up Internet service, which nobody misses.

Anyway, not only does this movie have great acting in it, but it has a great storyline too. In it, the biggest fear facing the character Meg Ryan plays is that a big discount bookstore, Fox Books, is moving to the block where her family-owned bookstore is already located. She decides that the best tactic is for her to fight for her business. Even though she begins to feel the fear of failure creep in, and her doors eventually close, she fights for her shop until the end. Her passion is clear in her attempt to save it.

I tell you this movie's storyline for two reasons. Yes, she pursued her idea because she had a passion for books and a passion for the business that had been in her family for many years, but the main point I want to convey is that things don't always turn out how you think they will. Some things in life just won't go as planned, but it's what you do with these moments that sets you apart. Meg Ryan's character didn't see that Fox Books would move in and ultimately destroy her family business, but that's what happened. She put up a good fight, but as we see in the movie, it wasn't enough. Was that failure? I don't think so.

Even though this example is from a movie, this is more or less what real life looks like. My life didn't go exactly as planned and I'm sure yours hasn't either. Even if you have already built a plan for your life, you can't see the future. You can try to predict it all you want, but there are just some things outside of your control. And even when things don't go as planned, you can always go back to the idea phase and start again. That said, it's a great practice to identify the things you *can* control in your bravery journey and to focus on them. This will allow you to stop focusing on the life happenings you have no control over. Try drawing a simple table in your notebook, to identify what is and isn't in your control, that looks like this:

| I HAVE CONTROL OVER... | I HAVE NO CONTROL OVER... |
|---|---|
|  |  |
|  |  |
|  |  |

Looking at this table alongside the chart you drew previously will help you have fewer headaches as you seek to find bravery with your ideas and will give you more power over your life. So the next time you need to decide between rising to the occasion or missing an opportunity, choose to rise and fight for what you believe in, because you do have control over that. You have control over your actions and your perceptions. And you definitely have control over the decision to fight for your ideas. You actually have more control than you think, even when you "fail."

## There's No Such Thing as Failure—Really!

Every time you dream up possible failures, those dreams put your fears on display. Maybe someone told you along the way that you should fear what might happen if you take action, and now you can't take action because you decided to believe in their fear of failure. Sure, the *fear* of failure is real, but *fear* is the only thing that makes it real, not failure. Please hear me out on this one.

In the biography by Frank Lewis Dyer, *Edison: His Life and Inventions*, Thomas Edison's associate, Walter S. Mallory, tells of an exchange of words between him and Edison after working on the development of a battery for more than five months, which has profoundly changed my perspective on the role mistakes and failure play in our personal growth and success:

> I found him at a bench about three feet wide and twelve to fifteen feet long, on which there were hundreds of little test cells that had been made up by his corps of chemists and experimenters. He was seated at this bench testing, figuring, and planning. I then learned that he had thus made over nine thousand experiments in trying to devise this new type of

storage battery, but had not produced a single thing that promised to solve the question. In view of this immense amount of thought and labor, my sympathy got the better of my judgment, and I said: "Isn't it a shame that with the tremendous amount of work you have done you haven't been able to get any results?" Edison turned on me like a flash, and with a smile replied: *"Results! Why, man, I have gotten a lot of results! I know several thousand things that won't work."*[1]

Edison is right: Mistakes are what allow you to fight the conventional thinking of "if something isn't broken, don't fix it." The fact that it has always been done one way doesn't mean it's the right way. You can use mistakes to analyze, tinker, and make things better than they ever would be without mistakes.

James Dyson, founder of the Dyson Company, has also adopted this mentality. He made 5,127 prototypes of his vacuum before he landed on a product that was right. It took fifteen years and many attempts before he came up with his final product, but he learned from every mistake along the way. James understood what it requires to find success, and the same applies to you.[2]

When I made the decision to attempt new things, I definitely made a few mistakes along the way, but that was never failure—it was learning. I found that when I made mistakes along my journey, my first inclination would be to call them "failures," but that wasn't true. Mistakes are boundary pushers that try to help you escape from the status quo. The power in making mistakes actually made me into something better than I was before. And sometimes it was in the very thing I was most afraid of failing that I found the most freedom.

## Relentlessly Chase Your Dream

After I began coaching other people, I eventually added business consulting to my services. This was after I had been in management for seven years with a company and had owned a business for some time. Of course, I'm not going to tell other people what they should do before I try it out for myself, and my experiences along the way have only given me better insight.

Anyway, if you haven't already figured out that entrepreneurs wear many different hats, then let me be the first to tell you that we all do. Given that 80–90 percent of new businesses don't work out, having many different businesses going at the same time may be a symptom of our own suppressed fears. If one business is going through a slump, then we always have a backup.

But if you ever want to start a business, know that it hardly ever takes off on its own, especially in the beginning. It's not as sexy as you think, and you may have to work two other jobs to find success. But if you are passionate about it, results will eventually come. They may not be the results you are hoping for, but you will learn some valuable lessons along the way. I can promise that.

When I first started my life-coaching business, I was afraid to tell people how they should live their lives, but I was more afraid of not pursuing my passion for helping people. (Originally I thought of pursuing other professions where helping people was the main focus, like becoming a guidance counselor of some sort, but becoming a life coach allowed me to own a business while doing what I loved.) The market was full of similar businesses, and people who had been doing it much longer than me were having immense success. Why would people listen to me?

As I was preparing for the launch of my new business, I remember calling a friend who was pursuing a very similar venture. Her name is Julia, and she was a writer for my team at that time, so we already had a good relationship. She always had great advice, so I began talking to her about the business I was dreaming up. I told her I would be doing some sort of consulting, but didn't know if I should lean toward business consulting or life coaching. I was qualified to do both, but didn't like the term "life coach," so I was leaning more toward business consulting. Funny that I was basing my decision on the title of my job, but, to be honest, I still don't like the term. I thought about telling people that I was a "people helper" and an "encourager," but those terms were too vague. I also came up with the term "life consultant," but that didn't work either.

We continued discussing what title fit me best. During that phone call, Julia helped me pinpoint my exact wants from the business by asking me one question: "What do you want to do?" This question was anything but simple. There was far more to it than meets the eye. I pondered the question for twenty-five seconds or so and responded, "I want to help people become better." And her response to my answer was, "Well, it sounds like you want to be a life coach, then." It made sense really. Everyone knows the term "life coach," and knows what they provide, so people know what I'm offering when they see that's what I do. Of course, being upfront with people about what I would offer them was great for marketing, and that made the decision even easier. "Life coach" was the title that stuck. For what it's worth, I have found that life coaching includes business consulting when the individuals I'm coaching own businesses, so I get the best of both worlds.

After the phone call with Julia, I used some tips from others who had developed a coaching business of their own. Then I worked with my brother-in-law to develop a form of the main tool I still use with clients to this day. I then attached all the information about my new business to my website, which my audience already visited on a regular basis. The final step was to tell others about my business, and a life-coaching business was born.

In the beginning, I was working away to help my business become foolproof for the future. To fight my fear of failure, I found that it was imperative to learn from people who had already been where I wanted to go. They blazed the trail for me and took the time to share their wisdom. It would have been dumb not to listen. To make better decisions, we must be willing to learn, not only from other people, but from the good and bad decisions we make along the way. We can learn from the victories and mistakes we encounter with our ideas, and it is up to us to remain teachable throughout the process.

## Continually Create Better Ideas

We can look at ideas from ten years ago and see that they are different from today's ideas in many ways. The opportunities that are available to us now come from a progression of technology over the past ten years, ten more years of research, ten more years of thinking up new ideas, and ten more years of testing our own limits. Your ideas right now are hopefully better than they were ten years ago. Ten more years of experience have influenced your ideas: ten more years of taking action, ten more years of joy, and ten more years of struggle. The more experience you have, the more ammunition you have to destroy the fear of failure.

You need to encounter every step for true bravery to appear, and each individual experience along the way helps shape the ideas you have. Who your ideas are for and what problems your ideas help solve depend on how you see the world at this moment in time. Your personal needs and wants will even help form better ideas, but it is where your expertise meets the needs of others that your ideas will impact the world. And when you have all the criteria needed to form a better idea, let that be sufficient reason to not hand the fear of failure a bullhorn.

Dare to dream ideas so big that they make your fear of failure pale in comparison, and then use your driving passion to fuel your pursuit. Doing this forces your creativity to shine and helps you find a way even when the fear of failure tells you otherwise. That's how you win time and time again. Even when the fear of failure screams loudest, know that the possibilities still remain endless.

The reason that there are so many different ideas is that we are all wired differently. Diversity fuels creativity, but what's even more remarkable is when people learn to collaborate. Collaboration takes your better ideas to the next level. So how does collaborating start? It begins with asking yourself the question, "Who else has the same idea as me?" When people ask this question and find other people to join them, ideas become bigger and spread faster. To take collaboration one step further is to ask the question, "Who has ideas that are different from mine?" Collaborating to form even better ideas comes from asking these questions, and better ideas are your best way to fight failure. Even when you don't know which way to turn next with your ideas, it will be creativity paired with passion and collaboration that will help you find bravery.

Throughout the process, know that very rarely is an idea sufficient on its own, because better ideas are meant to be built upon. If an idea comes to you, write it down to capture it, but don't consider it your final idea. Your ideas are meant to connect the dots, so others can enjoy your work. Very rarely are ideas completely original at first, but it is when you piece all your ideas that fit together into a package that you create an original and better idea.

Take the bravery process, for example. That in itself took months to pinpoint, not to mention the time that it took to discover the top ten fears that people face, and then to write the content for this book, and then to piece it all together. This book took years to create, but it would have taken much longer had I not developed an idea process that I use for all of my best ideas.

My own practice is to grab two ideas that have one similarity or more, to see how they relate and to see how they're different. Once I have an idea of how they fit together, I take two brand-new ideas that are completely different from the first batch, and then find something similar between those two ideas. Finally, I take the first set of ideas and the second set, which are opposite in some way, and try to connect the dots between the opposites—in this book, the two ideas are complacency and bravery, and the dots are the steps in between them. This process of creating is where creative, original ideas are born.

Yes, the idea process that I just described is time-consuming, but it's the only way to produce better ideas. At the core of making this process work is, of course, passion. You'll put in the work and time if you are passionate about your idea.

If you are passionate but still stuck about what to do next with your ideas, then the best thing to do is to work backward from where you are. Take the situation apart. What other angle can you look at your situation from? What other ideas are needed to see success? Your ideas don't need to be perfect, because being passionate about an idea is enough to start working toward bravery.

## The Antidote for the Plague of Perfectionism: Learning from Your Mistakes

As founder and CEO of BroadbandTV, Shahrzad Rafati says that she looks at every mistake as a lesson. She's become okay with making mistakes, and doing so has made her very successful. Instead of cowering from her mistakes, she wants to understand how her mistakes affect her business. Whether it's a significant error in judgment or a minor oversight, she strives to find value in every outcome. Shahrzad has found that perfection doesn't exist.[3]

The number one reason people give in to the fear of failure is that they can't seem to land on their preconceived idea of perfection. That's right; the fear of failure typically begins before you even start. Some people will never reach their full potential because of this false belief that perfection is somehow obtainable, but I agree with Shahrzad: perfection doesn't exist. Knowing this, we can fight the fear of failure by continuing without losing our passion, as we learn from each mistake we make along the way.

It is in this perseverance through the mistakes we make along the way that bravery is lived out. Once you decide that perfection isn't attainable, you learn to enjoy the process and to never stop improving. Stop being so hard on yourself, and know that making mistakes is just another part of being human. You don't have to be perfect to help people.

The question then becomes, what will you do with your mistakes? Will you sulk and go down with the ship or will you adapt to what life throws your way and rise to the occasion? The key to bravery is getting back up and trying again and again and again. So, what if we saw the act of getting up after making mistakes as the true start of learning? You can use your mistakes as stepping-stones to the next thing instead of seeing them as obstacles that stop you in your tracks. The choice is yours.

Because mistakes are inevitable, we need to learn how to embrace them. Stop allowing yourself to be caged in by perfection and instead start thinking of how you can change things through your messy mistakes. Bravery takes shape as we make mistakes in the areas we care most about, and learn from them. With mistakes, new possibilities often open wide, to bring success into reality. The willingness to make better mistakes gives you the freedom to pour your heart and soul into what you do.

Make glorious mistakes along the way, because a world without mistakes is a world without creativity, and that's a drab world nobody wants to live in. When you take the freedom to make mistakes, you will find that confusion can be turned into learning, sparking beautiful opportunities for potential, remarkable objects of creation, and continual reminders of why we create in the first place. We all can use our unique passions to embark on our very own creative journey. You are a genius, with passions and gifts only you possess. Be creative. Be you.

## Get Creative with Fear

When I started my life-coaching business, I hadn't constructed many life plans for others yet. (That's why I started that business while owning another one.) But I had done plenty of my own, year after year, so I knew what worked and what didn't. I was working toward making my business successful, but I needed practice before gathering more new clients and growing my business. So I did the most creative thing I knew to do, and I gave away twenty free consultations to anyone who was interested in bettering their life. (One of these consultations went to a plumber from Minnesota named Franklin, and by taking my advice, he landed a career that fit more into his passions.) Doing this gave me a future client base, kept me moving forward with my idea, and helped me find my bravest self.

Sure, I made the mistake of giving some bad advice in the beginning, like telling people that they could find the typical definition of work-life balance or that everyone needs to be a morning person, but my views have changed over the years. I've become wiser from my interactions with other people and so have you.

Becoming creative with your approach to life is the enemy of the fear of failure. When your current circumstances seem too difficult to face, complacency will keep you stuck in the fear of failure, and creativity is sometimes the only thing that will get you moving toward bravery. Allow the dam of creativity to burst wide open, and let the waters flow out of you and into what you're doing. When you allow your life to bleed this way, your mistakes eventually turn into triumphs. Fear of failure will attempt to put obstacles in the way of your ideas and out-of-the-box creativity, but you can put up a fight by getting comfortable with using your creativity on a daily basis. Let creativity be the paint for your life's canvas and begin forming the perfectly designed picture for your life.

Great examples of how the creative process works are all around, in the inventions geniuses have created throughout time. Can you imagine a world without lightbulbs? Can you imagine a world without telephones? Can you imagine a world without computers? Can you imagine a world without cars? Can you imagine a world without the bravery, research, and inventions of Edison, Swan, Maxim, Bell, Meucci, Babbage, and Benz? I can't.

These are people who took their own ideas and mistakes, and the mistakes of others, and made them into something remarkable. They learned that mistakes along the way would fuel their fight against the fear of failure and also elevate them and their ideas to new heights. Remember that everyone faces the fear of failure, and the best remedy is to make mistakes that encourage future breakthroughs.

In the process of creation, these inventors tried to build prototypes time and time again without success. Tens and hundreds and thousands of times they tried, with the passion and curiosity they had in their hearts, to turn their ideas into tangible inventions, but the fact is that each time they tried, they made astronomical numbers of new mistakes. But these inventors understood that even with passion in hand, perseverance is necessary. So they kept building on each mistake they made along the way, which ultimately produced the best possible product at that point in time. They knew they could help other people with their inventions, and they were ready to put in the work. Sure, there were days when each of them felt like giving up, but that's the beautiful thing about perseverance: a deep skill set is always secondary to someone's deep passion.

Perseverance is so important because success can only happen when you are willing to try and try again. Success relies on odds. The more times you fight your fear and show up, the better your chances are of finding success. If the results you are looking for aren't happening, it's very likely because you aren't showing up again and again. Are you having trouble showing up? If so, you need to find the passion to persevere.

It is much easier to teach someone the practical skills they need to fight fear than to teach that they need passion to fight fear, but both are necessary to success. If someone only possesses skills and doesn't get it right the first time, they will probably quit after that one attempt. But the person whose passion tells them to persevere will keep pushing through less-than-ideal circumstances until they achieve what they set out to do in the first place. It is passion for life that gives us perseverance, even when we are dealing with the fear of failure. Therefore we must dial in to our passionate being and become aware of its power.

Studies show that we can even increase knowledge and brain-power if we exercise our brains properly.[4] This is exciting news, because it means that we can grow in our creativity. We all have brilliant minds waiting to think up new ideas. The biggest problem is that many people aren't using anywhere near the amount of potential they have to create something amazing with those ideas.

Some people will blame this on the fact that they are geared one way, and one way only. They believe they can only be an idea person or a person who creates, but I would argue that both are incredibly important skills for any individual to possess. If you fear one and not the other, then you must fight for the other. The creation process is what gives you more ideas, and ideas are what make your creations better. This means ideas and creating go hand in hand. We must learn to live with both in our possession, using each to enrich our lives.

Don't let a few mistakes lead you astray from all the bravery you are producing in your life. When you allow this to happen, it kills every ounce of good momentum you have created. When you see that there is no right or wrong within creativity, you will be able to see the value in mistakes. When you change your perspective on your mistakes, they will look much more productive than they might have in the past. When there is no punishment for doing wrong in the creative process, open minds deliver contagious ideas, and it all starts with having the freedom to make mistakes.

## Mistakes + Creativity = Contagious ideas

It doesn't stop with you or me, but it does begin there. The only way to end with contagious ideas is to use creativity and mistakes to get us there. We need more ideas to spread, which means we need less fear of failure.

That said, here are two creative ways to fight fear and produce more contagious ideas right now:

### Strategy 1: If You Are Stressed Out, It's Time to Relax

Let's be honest. Everyone is stressed out these days, trying to meet heightened expectations. When everyone else is doing one thing, it takes creativity to go against the grain. Do you ever have to race to get things done because you started too late to complete what you needed to do? If so, that's not using your creative gift to its full potential. Being in a hurry takes your focus off the creativity waiting to be unleashed inside you. I know that when I am in a hurry, shortcuts sound appealing, and with deadlines looming, I cut out things that could have made projects better. But without time, something has to give. For the sake of saving time, creativity is the first to go. Just do what is required and move on is the name of the game. But when this is your approach, you aren't making yourself available to be creative, and you'll end up rushing through the important lessons that life needs to teach you.

You will be more creative when you have extra time and are open to possibilities, instead of being scatterbrained. Research even shows that the more we relax, the more creative we will be.[5] Instant gratification isn't all it's cracked up to be. Start early next time you are faced with a deadline, and give yourself a chance to be more creative with your work.

Something usually has to give when you pick up new things to do, but beginning anew doesn't always have to mean that other areas of life need to suffer. When we know what our top priorities are, we don't have to wonder what needs less attention, because we have already streamlined our life. When we take on anything and everything, life quickly becomes chaotic. I'm sorry to break it to you, but you can't possibly do everything in this world and still do it well. When you decide what to pour your heart into, you allow yourself to be more creative and can then make a bigger impact with your life.

Room to breathe is what will help you get the best work done. Deadlines do help us complete our work, but they don't help us produce our best work. Having more time and space allows for more tinkering with ideas. Great things happen when there is time to mold ideas into better ones, and that only happens when we give the process of finding solutions more of our time. Rushing creativity leads to basic thoughts, but when we have time to ponder those ideas, we push through them to find our best possible answers.

You can also increase creativity by learning to separate creating from editing. There is one part of the brain that carries out creativity and a different part of the brain that edits. You need to set aside separate time for each if you want to do creativity justice.

Get out whatever is inside of you needing to be created, and then come back later to fit the pieces together like a puzzle. This is my favorite part of creativity in the idea process, as there is no wrong. It is fun to work through this process, because you don't have to discard what you don't use. Whatever you create is useful, because you can save what you don't use for later, and use it for something else. No matter what you want to create, this often saves huge amounts of time down the road.

## Strategy 2: If Things Aren't Currently Working, It's Probably Time to Restructure Your Workflow

People need different amounts of sleep, have different careers, have different family situations, have different amounts of distances to commute, need different things from life depending on what life stage they are in, and yet I hear that people have copied the schedules and workflows of other people, thinking that they will somehow receive the same benefits. This makes absolutely no sense. One-size-fits-all advice hardly ever works, but creativity with your schedule and workflow does work. For this very reason, you may need to figure out what to do with your schedule on your own, and follow other people's advice in different areas. Sure, there are principles that can be applied to everyone's schedule, such as the need for a blocked-out time for meditation, but your day will look very different from everyone else's. It would be ignorant to think that everyone has a flexible schedule, works from home, or even that they work during the daytime.

Two years ago, I met an emergency room nurse who had hardly slept that week, and this happened often with her profession. If I would have suggested that she become a morning person or that she needed to find some sort of balance with her life in that moment, she would have either laughed at me or slapped me. Either way, suggesting a set schedule for someone else to follow without looking at their personal circumstances first is absurd. Stop following someone else's schedule hoping that it will better your own life. Have a better workflow by crafting your personal everyday systems and adjust them to fit your needs.

To find your best workflow, you must experiment, break a few things, and figure out what works. Making your workflow the best it can possibly be will free up valuable time to pursue passion in your work. And if you need even more proof of why this is important, studies show that people who are able to pursue their passions at work are five times more productive than those who don't.[6] If that doesn't sell you, I don't know what will.

Your workflow matters because your work matters. When you do anything less than your very best in your work, you end up having to convince people to buy your products. But when you produce great work, you can't wait to tell others about it, because you know they will love it and it will improve their lives. It's a win-win situation for everyone involved!

The issue could also be that you need to play around with your schedule so you are doing the right tasks at your peak time of day. An example would be to do the most important things first if you are a morning person and at night if you are a night-loving person. This is a practical but important example of how to use your creative juices well. Do work when you feel most productive and watch the quality of what you produce skyrocket.

Many times, people think that to be creative they must own or rent a cabin in the forest, lock themselves in a room, and come out only when they have produced their final piece of work. Or maybe you imagine splattering paint on a wall and staring at it until you see something. I don't mind cabins or paint splattering, but this isn't what everyday creativity looks like. In everyday creativity, a great place to focus is your workflow. You might be doing the right things but in the wrong order or not in the most efficient ways. Depending on the line of work you're in and what you are trying to accomplish, there may be better tools than the ones you are currently using to conduct research or even to do your job. Find what works and use optimum performance to fight the fear of failure.

Here are four questions you can begin asking to decrease your fear of failure, increase creativity, and better your work right now:

- How can I continually innovate with the ideas and the resources that I already have?
- How can I stay ahead of others, both inside and outside of my field?
- How can I become 2x more productive with my daily activities?
- How can I reach more people, both inside and outside of my current market?

Asking yourself these important questions will not only get your creative juices flowing but will help decrease your fears. Becoming better at anything and everything you possibly can will increase your confidence and exercise your bravery muscle. Creativity gets lost in the shuffle when people become comfortable with life. When individuals get into complacent routines, staying safe seems like the only reasonable answer. When this happens, people become satisfied with what life decides to bring them, and many times, these individuals come to the end of their journey, wondering where all their precious time went.

There is so much for you to explore and you have the capacity to do it well, but you have to take the time to dream it and grab hold of courage to make it happen. You should use your potential to the fullest and tap the creativity that's already inside you to fight your fear of failure, but don't expect to get it perfect the first time.

Much of creativity consists of attempts, but that is what keeps the process alive. Never stop attempting, never stop creating, and always remain curious about what this world holds. For when you lose curiosity, you lose passion. When you are curious, you ask better questions, leading you to discover the bravest you.

## Stay Curious and Do Some Research

Audrey Scott and Daniel Noll, a husband-and-wife speaking, writing, and photography team, have found ways not only to have fun but to turn their fears into curiosity about the world. They quit their secure jobs, sold everything, and set out on a new and exciting journey. Even after more than ten years, they're still pursuing their passions, curious about what the world has to offer. Sure, through all this they have had to face their fear of failure repeatedly, but they continue to be fueled by their hankering for newfound life experiences.

Lives like Audrey and Daniel's show how curiosity and creativity can work together when we allow them to. I'm sure people told them along the way that their dreams wouldn't become a reality, but they were passionate enough to discover bravery. Maybe your dream isn't to pick up and move so you can see the entire world, but regardless of what your dream is, a little creativity is sometimes the difference between finding bravery and getting stuck in complacency.

A good sign that you don't use enough everyday creativity is if you find yourself saying things like "that's not how I've done it before" or "that's not even possible." These statements are the enemy of making mistakes and fighting the fear of failure. Becoming curious about the world, and taking risks while making mistakes, says that you mean business and that you truly want to create good change. Fear likes to retract, but bravery pushes ahead and remains curious about the world. Yes, you will still pass through mountains and valleys on the way to where you are going—that comes with any journey—but you will be better for the journey in the end.

Now, I am not recommending that you just go start making wild guesses, hoping something will work. That will lead to frustration and, ultimately, to giving up. The only lesson found in doing that is what not to do next time.

Before tackling anything, you need to do some research and gain knowledge about the creative journey you will be embarking on. Doing this will show you what is required to fight your fear of failure and achieve your biggest goals. Who knows? You might do the research and find that you don't want to go after what you originally thought you wanted to pursue. Research helps you understand the reality of your dreams. Don't skip the research part of the journey, because you could save yourself avoidable heartache and boatloads of time.

These are some great research questions to begin with:

- **You may be pursuing your top goals, but is this the right season of life for you to go after them?**
- **What resources do you need to make your goals happen?**
- **How much time are you willing to give to make things happen?**
- **Is the journey worth the struggle?**

These are all important questions to ask yourself, and questions only you can answer. If you aren't able to give the answers you want to give, then you may need to change your course.

Have I personally gone after dreams and not achieved my desired results, even many years later? Yep. Have I spent time and money on projects I thought would work but ultimately flopped? Absolutely.

But they were all things I wanted to pursue because I was passionate about them, and even though they didn't work out as planned, I now have incredible stories to share about my journey.

## Have Fun in the Creative Mess

We should all have a passion for bringing creativity into our everyday lives, because not only does it fight failure, it's also just flat-out fun. It's difficult to be afraid when you're laughing, not to mention that when you're having fun, you're attracting more people because everyone wants to find out what you have and they don't.

OMNIGON, a nine-year-old digital consulting firm, is passionate about this idea of having fun. At OMNIGON, you have plenty of opportunities to spend quality time with others on your team, as well as the opportunity to spend fun time with clients. "The Fun Committee"—the people in charge of creating fun activities and experiences at OMNIGON—has been known to put together outings that include making build-a-bears and distributing them to a local children's hospital, and going to support their local professional sports teams. But the fun isn't confined to the fun committee—it truly is a part of the entire ethos at their offices in the United States, Canada, and Europe.

After researching countless fun companies, I now want to work with OMNIGON. I have friends who work for digital consulting firms, but they never rave about how fun it is. If anything, they sound depressed about their work environment. Even with most companies knowing the importance of fun and laughter, they have made their bottom lines their only focus, sucking the life out of their work and making their biggest fears their main focus. We need more laughter in our lives, not only because it is fun, but because numerous studies show it also relieves stress and increases risk taking. It will make your life better because it helps you fight fear!

An easy way to find creativity is in the midst of having fun. Being serious all the time is killing your creativity and your passion. Creativity thrives in the lives of those who know how to have fun, because the focus is not only on their art and work but on the joy behind it. If you're not having fun, chances are that burnout is close by.

It doesn't matter if I am talking about you as an individual or discussing the teams you collaborate with at work; either way you have a serious need for having fun. (The person who came up with the Color Run has to think the same way that I do.) Of course, we all experience fun and even live fun out in different ways, but we need to live in the place of happiness where we find joys in life, instead of always dwelling in the fearful pressures that can consume us. For me, I have some of my most fun moments with my work. I am grateful for the joy it brings, especially given how much work it takes to make businesses successful. But whatever it is that drives more fun and happiness in your life, discover it, and do it often.

If it is difficult to remember the last time you had fun, then you need to go on a journey to find fun once again. If you have never been able to enjoy having fun because you feel that you were made to grow up too quickly, or you have been more inclined to see negativity in the world, then it is time to find the joy that is already inside you. Even if it's a stretch, go back to the times when fun was a way of life. What was it that made you see the exciting fun in life? That's what you need to get back to. You need to get back to the fun found in life and creativity. There is beauty in both of these things, and when you combine them, there are endless possibilities.

## CHAPTER 5

# The Fear of Rejection

You have probably heard of J. K. Rowling. (If you haven't, you've been living under a rock.) She's the brilliant writer of the Harry Potter book series, which has sold millions of copies and has been translated into seventy-three languages, and has been adapted into phenomenally successful movies that have grossed over $20 billion at the box office. And that's only the tip of the iceberg.

After reading that paragraph above, I bet you would never guess that Rowling has dealt with crippling rejection in her life, unless you've done your research. In fact, her writing journey was anything but easy, but she followed her passion for writing and fought through her fears of rejection to find bravery.

While writing her first Harry Potter book, Rowling's mother passed away, and she had a baby and divorced her husband. Needless to say, writing the book was the last thing on her mind while dealing with everything else. While going through all this, she battled with depression too. But after completing her first manuscript, she battled her fear of rejection by sending it off to twelve different publishers. She was ready to hear back about all the work she had put into her story, but her readiness didn't seem to matter. All twelve publishers rejected the book. She was discouraged. Little did she know that an editor at Bloomsbury would find her book and champion her work, so that everyone could read Harry Potter.

Rowling understood what it meant to fight the fear of rejection. It took determination in the midst of adversity to find success, but we can all now see why she endured. The world needed her work, and her passion kept her going. The good news is that the same passion that was available to her is available to the rest of us, but it's up to us to embrace its benefits.

As Roald Dahl writes in *My Uncle Oswald*, "I began to realize how important it was to be an enthusiast in life. . . . If you are interested in something, no matter what it is, go at it full speed. Embrace it with both arms, hug it, love it and above all become passionate about it. Lukewarm is no good."[1] If we devote every ounce of passion to our lives, then we are living life in the way it was meant to be lived. Yes, rejection will come, even when we find passion and put in the work, but we should be most satisfied with giving life our all.

## What Looks Like Less Is Actually More

Years ago, during my own career transition, I was desperate to do something different with my life, so I found myself interviewing for every job that sounded remotely interesting. This was a discouraging process, because I knew deep down that I was settling for something less than what I wanted to do, just to have a job that would pay the bills. At each interview I went to, when they asked where I saw myself in five years, I would tell them the huge dreams I was chasing at that time, and that it was a process, but I was determined to see it through. Of course, these dreams involved my entrepreneurial aspirations, which would take me away from the company that I was interviewing with in two years tops. (This is probably why a previous employer told me that I was too honest, but you can't blame me for fearlessly dreaming out loud.)

Needless to say, each time I would give this answer I could see that the person interviewing me would become immediately discouraged. They needed someone who would come and work for them, do what they needed done, go home, and repeat that same routine endlessly. They needed more puppets to direct. I wanted to chase my own dreams and they wanted to recruit me to work full-time on theirs. They didn't want to hire someone who wanted to become an entrepreneur who wrote books, and I didn't want to do anything that my heart wouldn't be fully in. Needless to say, I didn't get any of the jobs I applied for. I couldn't blame them for their reasoning, but I wasn't passionate about acquiring a job. I only needed one until I figured things out. If these people were telling me that my plans didn't fit into theirs, it meant I would have to work on my own plan if I ever wanted to pursue my passions as a career.

I learned that if I wanted to get rejected less often, I should put my actions where my words were. I was good at voicing my dreams, but my actions weren't matching up. I needed to begin making smarter moves along the road to becoming an entrepreneur. I needed to steward each step of the journey better than I was, before pursuing my biggest dreams.

## The Power of Stewardship

Many times our fear of rejection comes from thinking that life is all or nothing. This couldn't be further from the truth. We need to do a better job of taking care of what we already have in our possession before we can expect to see bigger and better things happen. Many of our fears stem from not understanding the importance of becoming great with what we already do, so we can learn how to best handle our future endeavors. It is familiarity that can give us comfort with our current and possible future fears of rejection. This goes back to the principle that life is a journey, and we can't have the end result without first enduring the beginning and the middle.

It seems to me that not enough emphasis has been placed on this idea of becoming a good steward, and instead more importance is placed on what we might gain in the future. One of the best examples I have ever seen of someone who knew how to be a good steward in their life was my boss at my first job, Brandon. He is still to this day the best manager I have ever known. Brandon knew how to coach others to become better; he knew how to get great results; and he was also very personable with everyone. Because of this, Brandon was able to build trust and relationships with both the team and customers.

Looking from the outside, it didn't seem like he should be this far along in life. He was young, he really hadn't been in management for a long time, and he was attending grad school full time while working full time to pay for his schooling. But even with being pulled in every direction imaginable, he understood the importance of doing well with what he already had. He didn't let busyness deter him from pouring himself into the lives of others.

I knew he had something that I wasn't able to grasp at that time, but now I understand the difference in Brandon. He was being a good steward. He knew that he didn't have to go out and develop a bunch of different attributes: he was already enough. Even though Brandon was in a waiting season, he knew what it meant to be a good steward with what he already had, and it paid off. He eventually found bravery with his idea of owning a restaurant and is still running it successfully to this day.

But what about those who push against stewardship and chase after the trend of obtaining more, more, more? The want of something more isn't necessarily a bad thing, but when having more is *always* your focus, you miss out on each daily opportunity to use the talents and passions you already have. When your focus is on the present moment, you are able to give more of yourself to those around you, thus impacting more lives. Bravery is all about showing up, and that's what stewarding your life well allows you to do. When you understand the need people have for you, it becomes your responsibility to be a good steward and give life every ounce of passion in your possession. When you learn how to steward well, growth always comes.

When things are going great, you probably don't feel the need to be a good steward, because you can't imagine that you could make your life any better than it already is. But let me challenge you to not lose focus on the importance of stewardship, so you can continue to grow. In most cases, growth doesn't happen because people don't give their lives or their work their very best effort. Being a good steward not only maintains the great things you already have but will make you into something better.

Maybe you currently find yourself in the midst of waiting and are wondering if the next door will ever open. Maybe you are making plans and are getting ready to put the work in. Or maybe you are submerged in the trenches of your work right now, wondering when this pace will ever let up. Or maybe you are in the season of reaping the benefits of the work you have put in for so many years and are wondering what to do with all of it now. Plain and simple: being a good steward in every life season is what will keep you growing.

If you are currently in a waiting season or have been there at some point in life, you know just how difficult this season can be. It's a season when playing it safe and fear will both attempt to keep you distracted for far too long. But understand that waiting doesn't have to be as difficult as most people make it out to be. Waiting too often encourages keeping to yourself and settling into complacency, but at some point you have to move out of your comfort zone and dare to make a change. At some point you need to take action. You can use the waiting season as a time to step out and try something different.

There is no better time to plan your ideal life and all its intricacies than the waiting season. Once you do this, you can start moving through this season and get to the next. Time is too precious to waste. You can use your time wisely to impact others in huge ways, especially in the waiting season.

You can also steward your ideas by responsibly going after them. Ideas accelerate when they are put into a specific plan of action. Your plan is simply a means to achieve your ideas, but every inspiration starts with a huge idea burning inside you. You can be a good steward by taking responsibility now. Live your story, tell it, learn from it, and plan it out.

To form a plan for your ideas, you can use the information you've garnered from the exercises, and add action steps below the chart you created. To make your goals measurable, as SMART goals are intended to be, you should answer the questions "When?" "Where?" "How?" and "Who?" for each idea. This will allow you to be extremely specific with every area of life where you want to turn fear into bravery.

Within the practice of planning out your ideas, you get to see what you truly care about. You should pencil out each and every detail, even the gifts you want to bring out in others. After constructing your plan, remember that only having a plan is never enough. At some point you need to take action in order to move forward. It's the only way to grow.

In most cases, we already have what we need to fight fear, but we must learn how to see our fears for what they are, mold our weapons into something great, and stand unabashed with bravery in tow. In other words, you should focus first on making what you already have better. In doing this you will expand your reach and grow your work into something bigger. Growth is always a byproduct of producing great work. You can apply this principle to your own life, your own craft, and your own art.

I know the easy solution is to say that you can use mind over matter and just think these things into existence, but the truth is that putting hard work into the right things always wins. Why is this? Because work not only gets things done, but it gives you the required experience to become an expert. This means that if you work even ten more hours per week than you are right now, many times, you can see success sooner rather than later. Big dreams typically equate to a lot of work and small dreams equate to smaller amounts of work. I know this is really simple advice, but the size of your dreams always dictates the amount of work that you will need to put in.

Vanessa Quigley, the cofounder of Chatbooks, knows just how true this is. She started a business and had invested several hundred thousand dollars into it—and it was failing. She then began focusing on a second idea and that wasn't working either. But within two years of starting the third version of her company, she went from a stay-at-home mom of seven to selling one million units of her new product.

And you know what she credits her success to? Bravery. She didn't let her lack of business education, experience, skills, or network keep her from creating something that she believed in. Instead, she put the work in, and eventually saw the reward that comes from having a great idea. She chose to be brave and it paid off.[2]

I, myself, used to dream of the day that things would become easier, but that day never came, and it doesn't look like it will show up anytime soon. In fact, I don't know any successful people who aren't busy doing difficult work. I used to make excuses for why I couldn't be there for others, mostly due to a lack of time, but I hadn't yet discovered the power of being a good steward with my life. The fact is that there are still people I come in contact with every second of the day who need me, and I still have the same responsibility to be a good steward that I've always had. The difference is that I am more aware than ever before that people are more important than my fears could ever be. You can give away everything you have within yourself to others right now, so you know how to be an even better steward with huge opportunities in the future.

Yes, I am now busier with my family, I have more commitments, and I work more than I ever have before, but I have stopped making excuses about why I can't make the time for people. When others aren't my top priority, all the work I put in is in vain. Being a good steward in my life didn't just happen somehow. There came a time when I had to decide that no matter what amount of time I was given, I would use it to the best of my abilities to affect the lives of other people. I put aside every excuse that I found in fear and decided to be a good steward of my time, and you can make the same decision right now. Bravery is always a choice.

In most cases, your results will show if you are successful. If you know anything about business, then you know that looking at your profit-and-loss statements will show if you have been a good steward with your resources. If you are working on a project for the business you work at, then you know that the time you put into your project will show itself by displaying just how prepared you really are when it comes time to present. When you are a good steward of your financial resources, you know that it will show both in your expenditures and in your savings. When you steward your time well, the benefits will show in the number of lives you affect.

Being a good steward of our resources is what strengthens character and integrity within each and every one of us. Whether we are talking about work, time, or money, being a good steward sets us up for greater success. It shows that we are paying attention, that we care about our responsibilities, and that we want to do well with what we already have. Fear isn't as sticky when responsibility is present. Knowing what we need to do is sometimes the easiest way to let bravery win.

When is the last time you really thought about being responsible for taking care of what you already have and growing it into something better? When something is given to you and huge, new opportunities come into your life, take the responsibility to be a good steward of them. Once you do well with what you have now, more will come to you. That's a principle that has always worked, and one that will remain true until the end of time.

Sometimes it may seem easier to give something away, delegate it, or even forget about it, rather than being a good steward of it. The thing is that we usually have the seed already in our hands, but we may not have the right soil, water, and sunshine in our possession yet. If you can imagine planting a seed and taking care of it until it grows into a full plant or tree, this is what being a good steward looks like. When you live life well, you can know beyond a shadow of doubt that what you already have in the ground will eventually grow to be a beautiful life-giving plant.

Now that we have talked about what being a good steward means, how can you fight fear by stewarding your own life well? Maybe you need to stop asking investors to put money into something you thought of yesterday, and instead develop a sound plan that others can believe in before you try to make the huge sale. Or maybe you need to stop trying to run a marathon before you can run a mile. Fear thrives on trying to take too large of steps before understanding the fundamentals of stewarding a plan well. Bravery comes when life is taken gradually, stewarded well, and more thought is put into each step you take. Less can actually be more if you give it some time.

If you need to make a big sale, get really good at making smaller sales first. If you need to ask an investor for capital for your business, prove yourself with a smaller business and get really good at running it first. If you prove yourself with smaller things, not only will other people trust you more, but you will develop more self-confidence along the way as well. If you ask me to invest in your business, but you got a DUI last week, have a pet tiger and ten mistresses, and are an alcoholic, I'm going to think twice about trusting your judgment. It sounds to me like you need to get really good at managing your life before I can trust you with more.

But even when you start off small and do everything right, there is still a chance later on that you will settle for less. Why is this? Because many times people will succeed at the wrong things and get in so deep that they decide to stay stuck.

Does "I'll stay put because I only have fifteen more years until retirement" sound familiar? I know I've heard people say that before. These people were probably told by other people that they would make a good _____ (fill in the blank), and, based on a few talents and congratulatory remarks, they followed the voice of the crowd. But now they are wondering whether they should stay put or leave for something better, while knowing they may be rejected if they try to leave.

If this is you, of course I can't tell you what to do. Every situation is different. But what I can tell you is that many times, people can find passion for the life they have or the work they do, no matter the situation. But you must change your outlook from one of hopelessness to one that sees the potential in your definition of bravery for things to change for the better.

People stay put when they begin settling for less and have lost a fascination with what they are doing. When we don't care about the outcome, we don't put forth our best efforts and don't care to find passion for what we are doing. The fear of rejection will cause you to get less from life, because you will stop attempting new things and will ultimately never be able to find bravery. Don't fall for the lie of rejection. Begin stewarding yourself well: learn how to do a better job with what you already have.

## Be Comfortable with Rejection

Throughout this book, I have conveyed the honest message that fear will come, and the fear of rejection is no different, but there is hope. We can learn how to overcome the fear of rejection by becoming comfortable with the rejection we will face in our lifetimes. If you've never been rejected, you've probably never put yourself in a position to be rejected, and that tells me that you're not taking enough risks. So here are five questions you must answer before we go any further:

1.  **Have you ever been rejected?**
2.  **If so, how many times?**
3.  **If so, why do you think you were you rejected?**
4.  **If so, did you do everything in your power not to be rejected?**
5.  **On a different note, how many times have you thought you would be rejected and weren't?**

The first four questions deal with actual rejection, and the last question deals with the *fear* of rejection. The answers to these questions will hold a lot of pain for many, but if you want to fight fear, it is necessary to look at the entirety of your life. The moment you no longer fear looking at both the good and bad moments in life is the moment you find the bravest you.

I can't tell you how many times I've been rejected, but each experience has made me stronger. In fact, a few years before writing this book, I submitted another manuscript to publishers that was terrible. I threw it together and didn't make any edits. The idea was three hundred pages of vagueness. And you want to know what happened? I lost count at twenty publishers rejecting it, and I then went back to the drawing board. Even though I was battling the fear of rejection with my first manuscript, the idea wasn't ready, and I wasn't ready either. I learned something very valuable through the book-writing process, and that is that if I'm not willing to put the work in, the results won't match my desired outcome, and the same goes for you.

When you are able to make the quality and quantity of work you put into things more important than your fear of rejection, you will be able to beat the fear of rejection. When you have put your all into something, you can know that you have done everything in your power, and you can then let go and allow others to fully receive what you have to offer. It's amazing to see that when people are able to let go and pursue bravery, things naturally seem to take care of themselves. This is because fear is only as powerful as your unfamiliarity allows it to be. And the only way to become more familiar with your fear of rejection is to put the work in.

To fight my own fear of rejection, I spent months developing the idea for this book, hired an editor I worked with for another four months, studied other writers, took a year to research more on fear than people would probably care to know, developed my writing even more, said no to various speaking engagements and business opportunities to devote more time to this idea, and then wrote this book. And you want to know what happened in those three years of concept to completion? I became a better writer, and, as a result, my dream publisher took notice of my work. I learned that when you decide to face the fear of rejection with hard work, it pays off. Don't ever let anyone tell you otherwise.

## Get Better at Asking

Author and entrepreneur Jason Comely came up with a game called Rejection Therapy, to help him fight the fear of rejection. The game requires him to ask strangers for certain things and to be rejected at least once a day, because it helps him face his own fear of rejection. He used exposure therapy—exposure to a feared object without any real danger—in order to overcome anxiety and to become comfortable with talking to people and asking them for things.

Jason's game is good at getting one comfortable with one's fear of rejection. It works with the possibility of rejection in both the small things and the big things in life. We can actually use what we learn from this game to become better at asking. The way we approach people, the way we communicate, and the way we view ourselves all show how we will stand up to rejection.

So how do we become better at asking? We combine our needs with the needs of others. When you ask for something to benefit yourself only, many times it is selfishness. When you ask others for something that helps everyone involved, including yourself, it is beneficial. And when you ask someone something to only benefit them, it is a form of gratitude.

Fear of rejection has a way of telling us that we can't do something because people will judge us for it, but the more often we do it, the more we realize that people aren't the gatekeepers to our fears—we are. When you become too comfortable and let fear keep you safe from rejection, the objects of your fear only seem more daunting. Passion tells you the opposite of everything fear tries to tell you. So when you find yourself running away from your fears, put yourself in the hands of passion. Fear will tell you all the reasons you can't, and passion will tell you all the reasons you can.

## CHAPTER 6

# The Fear of Missing Out

In 2008 social media was new to me. While trying to build some traction online, I was consumed with paying attention to the latest social media, business, and marketing trends. At some points along the way, social media was becoming such a distraction that I found myself feeding the addiction that 56 percent of people deal with—the fear of missing out, known online as #FOMO.[1] Social media was doing the very opposite of what it was intended to do, which is to connect people; it was disconnecting me from the people and world around me. (Relationship tip: if it's difficult to have a conversation because your face is always buried in a phone, it's time to set boundaries for your phone.)

So to fight my fear of missing out I did the only reasonable thing I could think of to bring the importance of relationships back to the forefront; I quit social media. The first time I felt the need to do this, it ended up being a month. The second time, it ended up being three months before I used it again. The third time, I didn't use social media for almost an entire year. During these times, I occupied myself with things that matter more than social media: things like my family, my friends, and my work. In doing so, I saw the importance of not comparing myself to everyone else, I increased my focus and my productivity, and I saw just how powerful hard work can be when one is able to work through one's fears.

Social media isn't necessarily a bad thing, but just as with anything in life, good things can become distractions when we use them in the wrong ways. In today's world, people have allowed their sense of self-worth to be contingent on how many likes and shares they receive on their social media accounts. And with Instagram helping people build up fairy-tale lives, who knows where this falsehood could lead? I mean, how many people give in to fear and deny telling the truth these days? How many people deal with a lack of confidence? And how many people truly open up to other people? Whether people want to admit it or not, real relationships are a very hard thing to build online, because of the lack of face-to-face interaction. In fact, my belief is that there will never be anything to replace the genuine interaction that happens when people are able to discover each other with nothing in the way.

You can tell if you are fearful of missing out if you are constantly wishing that you are somewhere other than where you are right now. The fear of missing out is a distraction from forming lasting relationships, because it keeps you focused on what every other person in the world is doing, rather than on the people right in front of you. The travesty spawned by this fear is that you forget to look to your right and your left and see the many people who need you in this moment. Your family, your close friends, your neighbors—they all need you to be present in this moment. And while being concerned with every person in this world is admirable, you don't have a constant, direct impact on those people. You are only one person. So instead of letting your fear of missing out put your focus on every other place in the world besides where you are right now, you can fight this fear by slowing down and focusing on the people you come in contact with every single day.

So, what's the best way to slow down in a world where everyone is trying to capture your attention in hopes of selling their products to you? How do you slow down when it seems that everyone expects more from you? How do you get rid of the distractions? The answer is minimalism. And I'm not just talking about minimalism in the sense of material things, which you are probably aware of; I'm talking about adopting the idea of minimalism in every aspect of your life. This is the difference between the fear of missing out and knowing that you're exactly where you should be.

## The Importance of Minimalism

Creative author and choreographer Twyla Tharp believes that the gods give infinite resources to those they wish to destroy.[2] We need minimalism in our lives to reduce our options, to increase our focus, and to make it easier to find bravery. Fear thrives when we give ourselves too many options, and this is where minimalism can help us tremendously.

When most people think of minimalism, they think of an office that has nothing on the walls and spotless desks. This is a good place to start, as there are three hundred thousand items in the average American home, but there's more to it than that.[3] If it is easier for you to conquer physical things first, and then go on to tackling the other ways you can implement minimalism into your life, then do it that way. You can start with the physical clutter that you see around your home and office. Once you have your physical space where you want it to be, then begin focusing on the things that take up your time and your mental space. This is what I really want you to focus on. I want you to take the mental picture of minimalism you have and to apply it to what you *do* every day. The fear of missing out loves distractions, so it takes bravery to rid yourself of the intangible things that clutter your life.

The whole point of minimalism is to create more room in your life so you can then add things to your life that matter. This requires constant pruning. I do it on a monthly basis in my own life. My friend Bob even prunes things out of his life on a weekly basis. Whether it's monthly, weekly, or daily, find what works for you, and use minimalism to help you fight your fear of missing out.

The lie that fear will feed you is that if you get rid of things in your life, you will miss out on something. You end up feeling forced to keep everything, and then to add more on top of it. If you prune back, you may indeed miss out on something, but those things will almost certainly be the ones that don't matter. You won't even miss them, because you only discard unimportant things when you adopt minimalism. Think of the time you don't seem to have to give to the people you love: a minimalist approach to life fixes this problem.

For you to overcome the fear of missing out, you must become laser-focused on what you want from life, and that's exactly what the minimalist approach offers. The biggest benefit of minimalism is that it makes focusing on the right things easier. To know how I'm doing with minimalism, I have come up with a return-on-investment assessment that shows me if I am using my time well. I've used it, and

I have also taken other people through this assessment to help them adopt a more simplistic view of life. It combines the number of lives changed, the shortest amount of time used for the most benefits received, and the return on investment gained from the amount of work you put in. If all we need to do is focus on three aspects, fear diminishes, and that's exactly what minimalism offers.

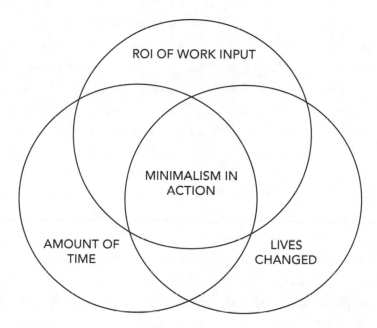

To find the sweet spot for minimalism in action, you must ask yourself, "How can I be passionate with my valuable time and impact the most lives possible?" If you want to apply this to business, the best question to ask is, "What passion can I pursue with my valuable time to affect the most lives possible while being the most profitable?" The answers to these questions will show you exactly what you need to be working on, and the enemy to following through, here, is distraction in all the forms that will come along the way.

Adopting this filter will tell you what you need to add to your life and what you need to drop.

Let this idea of minimalism be your filter when confronted with the fear of missing out. If you find that something doesn't fall in your sweet spot, then it's not worth pursuing. If you haven't thought of minimalism in this way before, you're not alone. The minimalist approach isn't adopted often, because people want more, and they want it now. Most people find themselves consumed by a busy lifestyle and want a way out, but they keep adding more, to feed heightened expectations, rather than setting boundaries and throwing the need for self-assessment out the window. This has to change.

When we make minimalism a way of life, we take the time that we were devoting to unimportant things and put it into what matters most. How can you get rid of things in your schedule so you can enjoy more time with your family and spend more time pouring into the lives of other people? How can you also reduce your commitment to things that either don't interest you or aren't productive? Your answers are found in minimalism.

Taking a minimalist approach to your life lets you free up time in every area of life, allowing you to recharge as well. When you're not afraid of missing out, you can stay in a continuous state of rest, which many of us desperately need. You can be more relaxed and remain focused on the things in front of you, rather than thinking about being somewhere else. I mean, what's the worst thing that you will miss out on? When you truthfully answer this question, you will see that very rarely will you miss out on anything that's more meaningful than what you are currently facing. You can choose to be present in the now, which is what everyone wants and needs from you.

## Practice Meditation

A great way to begin your day is with practicing the art of meditation. I start off every day with meditation—sometimes a short amount of time and sometimes longer—because it provides a moment of clarity. Maybe you don't like quiet because it makes you feel uncomfortable or alone, but this can be a sign that you are holding on to the fear of missing out. Only when you are comfortable with yourself can you be comfortable with the world around you.

Meditation can help realign you with your own needs and can also help you better see the needs of others. This world will speed you up and never let you think for yourself if you allow it to, but meditation can help ground you in the midst of chaos. The fear of missing out will make you want to keep going, often without any clarity about where you're going or why, and movement without understanding isn't often the best way to go.

Most people will tell you to keep taking action until you find what works, but we have forgotten the importance of using the knowledge we already have, of taking everything into consideration and then making a move. Sure life is fast paced, but we need to learn how to slow down. Sometimes you will need to assess the situation before making a move, and that's okay. Waiting to assess realistic outcomes is part of good planning. Once you see the outcome you like best, you will know which way you should go.

## Stop Comparing Yourself to Others

As I told you earlier, wrongly comparing myself to others is something that I've dealt with before. Comparison is always used as a distraction from taking a much-needed look at one's self. United States President Theodore Roosevelt is even thought to have said, "Comparison is the thief of joy," and I have to agree. When I compare myself with others, my fear of missing out distracts me from focusing on what I need. And while focusing on others is important, knowing how you are wired and what you need to succeed is extremely important as well.

For example, I'd like to talk a bit about sleep. I know a few entrepreneurs who feel great getting only three or four hours of sleep a night. Yes, I regret that I have compared myself to others in this area. This was before I realized that we only compare ourselves to others when we don't see that our passion shows us the way and helps carve out our purpose in the world. Another person's sleep patterns aren't going to help me pursue my passion, but I digress.

I feared that these sleepless entrepreneurs were getting more done than I was, as I need at least seven and a half hours of sleep to perform at my best level. Seeing that their productivity levels were higher than my own, I attempted to cut my sleep in half. I tried making my days longer by staying up to work later and waking up early to get a head start, but let's just say that it didn't work for me at all. I was angrier, less focused, and more tired than ever before. I quickly realized that changing my sleep pattern due to the fear of missing out was nonsense. We are all built differently and need different amounts of sleep.

According to the National Institutes of Health, the average adult sleeps less than seven hours a night, but most people, myself included, need 7.5–9 hours of sleep. Getting the correct amount of sleep can help improve your memory, increase creativity, maintain proper weight, lower stress, and can even contribute to living a longer life. When I found this out, I began studying REM sleep and how a good night's rest can positively affect a person's energy throughout the day.

I found that sleep follows a predictable pattern, moving back and forth between deep sleep and REM sleep. Together, the stages of REM and non-REM sleep form a complete sleep cycle. Each cycle is about ninety minutes, and the cycle repeats four to six times over the course of a night. It is important to realize this, because waking up just thirty minutes early, or even thirty minutes late, can drastically improve the way you feel and will help you pursue passion with greater tenacity.[4]

I found that instead of comparing myself to others, it was more important to get the correct amount of sleep for my body. A good rest was the fuel I needed to help me through each day, and maybe you're the same way. We will all get more done when we give ourselves the right amount of sleep and allow ourselves to rejuvenate. It's very difficult to be passionate about life when we are tired, so give yourself permission to sleep longer, and use that energy to fuel your passion. When we don't pursue our passions, it is a letdown, not only for ourselves, but for those around us, and even for people we don't know yet. This is what missing out actually looks like.

## Saying Yes or No

As you continue to become more passionate and successful, you will have to tell people no more often. There is only so much time in a day, and distractions will come your way, so saying no is the only solution you are left with. And many times, saying no is the bravest thing you can do. This was very difficult for me to understand at first, as I didn't like missing out on anything. But as I found myself stretched time and time again, and mentors even began telling me that I needed to let things go, I reluctantly began saying no more often. It was freeing, because when I said no to someone, I made sure they knew it was only for that particular event, and I could possibly make it work in the future. This allowed me to keep doors open for the future, and relationships healthy in the process.

In a recent interview, I was asked how I choose between the things that I say yes to and the things I say no to. I know this is a question you have pondered too. The answer lies in these five questions:

1. **Will saying yes make me wish I had said no later?**
2. **Is it inconvenient, and if it is, how come?**
3. **What could I be doing right now that is more important than this one thing?**
4. **How many chances will I have to do this one thing?**
5. **Is it detrimental to my health?**

Once I have weighed my answers to each of these questions, I then answer yes or no based on what the opportunity is worth to me. If you're like me—a recovering people-pleaser—then you know how difficult it can be to say no, so that's why I came up with this five-question filter before I answer yes or no. The answers to these questions can help you save time and will keep your priorities in line along the way. If the answers aren't what they should be, then you should move on to your next adventure. If the answers look good, then what are you waiting for? Say yes and fight the fear of missing out by showing up. It's time to take action and to tell other people about the dreams you are chasing.

## Buy into Your Huge Ideas and Communicate Them

Instead of telling you that you should only chase big ideas, which I would say is true, I want to show you the natural consequences of chasing both big and small ideas. You need huge ideas to make a huge difference. A huge idea is something so big that you look forward to meeting it with the sunrise each morning, or fall asleep with on your mind every night. Small ideas produce small amounts of influence, but don't require as much work. If you want to leave a small impact on this world, then have at it, but if you want to produce lasting change with your life, what you need are bigger ideas and the willingness to put in the work.

Once you buy into your ideas, the next most important step is to communicate those ideas to others. Let's first look at the need to articulate your huge ideas to your family. It's important to remember throughout the bravery process that your family is there to help you, not to squash your ideas. When Jasmine and I first got married, I got this all wrong. I looked at my ideas as mine alone, and not both of ours. I wasn't letting people in, not even my wife, and it caused tons of problems. I spent way too much time chasing these ideas instead of chasing her, and as a result, my selfishness made my marriage suffer. I was too busy chasing things rather than helping people. I have learned so many lessons in my marriage, but this one takes the cake. The lesson I took away from that experience is that no idea is worth pursuing if it will cost you a relationship. When I changed my actions to be in line with this perspective, I began impacting more people with my life. If this is something that you want to achieve with your life, the only requirement is that you put others first, but don't neglect yourself during the process of chasing bravery.

Once I changed my outlook from one of selfishness to one that valued teamwork, and communicated every aspect of my ideas to Jasmine, she was more on board than ever before. I didn't have to persuade her, but I did need to give her all the details. Knowing the details, both present and future, is a priority for everyone involved. When your family, friends, employees, coworkers, and bosses know why you are doing what you are doing, they will see just how important it is for you to follow your dreams.

Now that you have what you need to fight the fear of missing out, don't worry about what's ahead. Worrying about the change ahead does nothing but rob us of the present joy we could and should be experiencing. As my grandmother used to say, "Worrying doesn't do anyone good." And if you're worried about another kind of fear, by the time you get to the end of this book, you'll have everything you need to fight fear and become the bravest you.

## CHAPTER 7

# The Fear of Change

The idea of the future is my driving force. After taking various self-assessments, this is what I have found to be most true about myself. It's truly my blessing and my curse. Actually, I could have skipped the tests, because I didn't need books or some software program to tell me who I am. It's how I am built, so I've had to learn how to look at what is happening in the present moment in order to apply the practice of gratitude in my life. Being grateful for what has happened in the past and being thankful for what's to come in the future is what opens doors. However, looking too much at the future can unintentionally wire us to become selfish, and can lead us to forget how grateful we should be for opportunities to change things that aren't going so well. Not to mention that focusing too much on the future can also make you give in to fear before you even take the first step.

So how did I teach myself to be grateful? I stopped feeling entitled.

Entitlement is such a cancer, because it is void of gratitude. And once gratitude is gone, everything becomes about you. "I did this, so I deserve that" becomes a familiar way of thinking, and the negativity and bitterness that comes when something doesn't go your way will be detrimental to your success.

Gratitude, then, is the cure to entitlement. Where should one start with gratitude? Realize that life is a gift. That's why second chances and new sunrises are so beautiful. There's much to be grateful for.

I also learned to be content with being present in the now. You're probably thinking that contentment sounds terrible, and have always believed that you should never be completely happy with what you have. All driven people are supposed to be unhappy until we finally reach our goals, right? And once we have found the bravery to fulfill our ideas, we're supposed to move on to the next thing and start again. That sounds like a terrible life if you ask me. The problem is that passion will fade away in the monotony of the process if we try to keep up a maddening pace. This is why I believe the fear of change mainly stems from lack of contentment and gratefulness for life.

It is only when we learn to be content that we can look at change as new opportunity and fresh experience. In fact, we will actually be grateful for any good change that comes when this shift takes place. So please don't treat "contentment" as a disgusting word but rather as a word that brings peace in the midst of change. However, the word you should avoid having any part of is "complacency." The difference between these two words is significant. "Complacency" means you are satisfied with doing nothing, while "contentment" means that you are satisfied while doing something. As you can see, the two are very different. We must find the happiness and satisfaction contentment offers if we are to find inner peace and passion even when everything else is changing. Worrying about change ahead does nothing but rob us of the present joy we could and should be experiencing. Yes, life is ever-evolving, so we do need to prepare for the future, but this should also remind us of the need to take life as it comes, one day at a time.

## Do What You Were Wired to Do

The late entrepreneur Steve Jobs asked himself one very important question every day, and it's a question we all desperately need to be asking ourselves: "If today were the last day of my life, would I want to be doing what I'm doing?"[1] He understood the power of contentment as well. He followed this by saying, "Whenever the answer has been 'no' for too many days in a row, I know I need to change something." Jobs also viewed change as an opportunity to do the work he was designed to do. You should ask yourself the same question, because it requires you to become laser-focused on what you do in life, and this is never a bad thing. Sure, there will be a lot of work along the way that won't be fun, but if the core reason you do what you do doesn't matter, then you need to decide if you're in the right place.

I've lost sight of my purpose before, and the results were awful. The terrible thing is that it happens to so many people. When you don't know your purpose, your passion for life is lost, and a life without passion is a life with little hope. Your purpose wakes you up in the morning, your purpose increases your determination, and your purpose helps you find your way. The good news is that everyone has a specific reason they were created.

But even when you grab hold of why you are living and breathing, life isn't pure bliss all the time. The old saying "You don't work a day in your life when you enjoy what you do" sounds good, but it just isn't true. I love being an entrepreneur, but I still have to do paperwork and gather tax information, which isn't fun for me, but it's necessary. (It's absurd to me that some accountants actually like doing taxes. If that's you, then you truly have a gift.)

There are also meetings I attend and phone calls that I have to take that aren't the most fun, but they are necessary, as they quickly inform me of what I need to know. Honestly, I've found that there are aspects of owning businesses that aren't always fun and that I don't see an immediate return from, but such is life.

There are some things you will love to do, and some things you won't on your journey of chasing your ideas. Find passion for life, and choose to make the best of everything you do, including the activities that are less than desirable. If you don't want to be stuck doing things you don't enjoy, you can hire more people, delegate those activities, or find the purpose for what you need to do, and then do it.

Having a passion for life and knowing why you do the work you do can motivate you to do the stuff you wish you didn't have to do along the way. Every action needs a purpose, so when you decide to look at the reason why you do what you do, you will be able to see the not-so-fun tasks along the way with a different perspective. You can then analyze any problems you have with the process and find solutions to make it better.

But I want to challenge you on your priorities here. When people are the reason why you do what you do, you will make better decisions, you will create a better work environment for everyone, and you and your team will make better products. When you use your purpose as a filter, you allow it to control every word you speak and every action you take. It's that powerful!

## Listening to Your Purpose Will Tell You What You Really Want

The only people who don't care about having a passion for their purpose are those who have never experienced it. Once you find it, and feel what it's like to walk in it, you'll never be able to go back. Even when you step out with ideas, sometimes being brave and trying to change things will show you what you don't want.

I discovered this truth when I had a job interview with a publisher. I pursued the idea of working for a publisher because I love to write and wanted to understand the industry more, so it felt like a good fit. But when they began telling me about the job itself, it sounded more like the one thing I knew I didn't want to do—occupy a cubicle.

I had this mental image of what it would be like to work for a publisher, and it seemed great, but the lady interviewing me ruined the idea. She was condescending to me through the entire process, and for that I am forever grateful. She allowed me to see beforehand that it would have never worked out, so it was actually a gift. Since my interview didn't go well, I decided to do something different with my life. Shortly after that, I started my first business and began working on my first manuscript. I always wonder about that interview and where I would be if it had gone well. But the beautiful thing about "what ifs" is that they didn't happen, so I don't have to worry about them.

Of course, none of this would have happened if I had remained complacent and not bothered with finding bravery. I am reminded of the famous quote "Courage is not the absence of fear but the mastery of fear." Comfort is always found in safety, and the discomfort of fear is always there before taking a leap with passion for your ideas, but you must learn how to master the fear of change. That's your only hope for perseverance through difficult times.

## The Power of Quitting (Yes, It *Can* Help You Succeed!)

I thought I was having a heart attack. We were headed to a Colorado Rockies baseball game, trying to take my mind off of everything else happening in my life, but the fun wouldn't last long. The feeling came on me like a flood—I couldn't breathe, I couldn't talk, and I couldn't focus—I thought I was going to die. We couldn't get to the hospital fast enough. When we finally arrived, I remember stumbling to the receptionist desk, and barely being able to voice what was happening. I told her I thought there was a problem with my heart, so they ushered me to a back room immediately. They hooked me up to a bunch of beeping machines to check my status, and fortunately it wasn't a heart attack, but it was a panic attack. It was induced by high blood pressure, which was caused by my crazy schedule at that time. My intentions were good, but my execution was not.

In those moments of lying on a cold metal table, not being able to catch my breath, I will never forget the words that kind nurse spoke—"Just breathe, Adam." She was voicing the very problem I had with my life—I had squeezed it in such a way that I left no room to breathe. I didn't need the Diazepam they prescribed me to cope; what I needed was margin. My schedule had gotten out of control because I was scared of quitting something—anything, really—and I didn't want to let anyone down. But for my health's sake, I knew something had to give. So, I did the only thing I knew to do in order to recover quickly: I got rid of everything that I didn't *have* to do. I emptied my schedule bucket and started over, and it was the best thing I ever did.

Only putting things back into my life that I was required to do gave me fresh purpose, and has been the most effective move I have ever taken with my schedule.

From that time in life I learned that knowing one's limits, knowing how to make the most out of each and every day, and understanding what quitting can actually do for someone is imperative to have success. You can always oppose the fear of change with consistent perseverance, because when you are consistently relentless through difficult times, the end goal is solely contingent on your passion and endurance, but continuing no matter what isn't always the best answer. Sometimes the best answer is to quit. If you choose to quit, know that quitting isn't always rooted in fear; sometimes it's the smartest answer you have available. Sure, quitting brings about change, the one thing that so many people are afraid of, but if nothing ever changes, then you will always be stuck.

There are many people who want to make a dent in this world for the better, but either don't know where to begin or are just talk. Whether you fall into one of these groups of people or not, please understand that you still have time to make a difference. If you started along your journey with a heart bursting with anticipation for what would happen next and you were detoured by your fear of something bad happening somewhere along the way, I would recommend that you go back to the last moment you felt a passion for what you are currently pursuing. When you understand that it requires you to search out that same passion you had for the world, you will regain the same feelings that accompanied it, and the emotions that it brought to you when you used to enjoy it. But if that doesn't work, you can use quitting as a last resort, and take the permission to have fun so your passion for life can come once again.

Learning to quit the right things in the right way is especially important for those who can never seem to find enough time for the things they truly care about. Time is one of your most valuable resources, and some seasons of life will allow you to do more than others will. There is only so much time in the day, and there is only so much that can be done, so creating more time and using time wisely are the only ways you will ever accomplish more. Having room to breathe is important, not only because it makes you feel better, but because it gives you time to process the things that are important to you. Many people encounter a life that is far too full of both important and unimportant things, and if this sounds like you, quitting some of those things is your best and only option.

Before I explain this reasoning further, you must get over the preconceived idea that quitting is always a bad thing. Many people look at quitting as "throwing in the towel," but quitting isn't necessarily giving up. When quitting is done correctly, it's making room for something better. In fact, quitting is only natural. This is because as our lives continue we tend to add things on top of the basic priorities we already have. As things seem to get out of control, our priorities don't typically change, so we need to learn how to best maintain our schedules while letting certain unimportant things go simultaneously.

For many of us, the easy thing to do is to add more, right up until the point where we become desperate to slow down. But when we learn the much more difficult practice of proactive quitting, we never have to fear that we are living an unbalanced life. Instead of waiting for the fear of change to arise, you can fight it beforehand by routinely quitting what is unimportant and replacing those things with what *is* important for the season you find yourself in. This way, your life is comfortably changing regularly, and the process is happening naturally, rather than being forced.

A practice I have found useful is quitting twice the number of activities I begin. Doing this automatically gets my schedule back to where it should be and reminds me what my priorities are. As with adopting anything new, there will be a learning curve, so quitting more than I am starting gives me ample time to learn what I need to and gives me the chance to adjust to unfamiliar changes.

Sure, there are times when you have quit right before you've seen success, but evaluating each situation will let you know whether it was something you should have pursued in the first place. I want to help you with this necessary discovery of what you need to quit, whatever stage of life you are in. Quitting the old to find the new is necessary to fight your fear of change.

So here are eight signs that it may be time to quit something to make room for something better:

### Warning Sign 1: It's Damaging Your Health and Relationships

As many times as I have started something new, I have also had to know when to quit. Anyone can start something, but quitting gracefully is a true art. If you quit too early, you will miss out on the full benefits of embarking on the journey in the first place. But if you quit too late, stress levels will soar, your mental and physical health will diminish, and burnout will ensue. I can promise you that because I have experienced it firsthand.

If it is work-life balance you are worried about, you're not alone—70 percent of people can't find work-life balance.[2] But the reason for this may not be what you think. People cannot find work-life balance because the traditional definition of it doesn't exist. The key word we need to define before digging into what work-life balance looks like is "balance." Balance is *an even distribution of weight* enabling someone or something to remain upright and steady." Now, ask yourself the question, "Do I put the same amount of time into work as I put into living life?"

As Alain de Botton, who writes about philosophy and everyday life, says, "There is no such thing as work-life balance. Everything worth fighting for unbalances your life."[3] Retired business executive Jack Welch writes, "There's no such thing as work-life balance. There are work-life choices, and you make them, and they have consequences."[4] And executive Sheryl Sandberg says, "So there's no such thing as work-life balance. There's work, and there's life, and there's no balance."[5]

Heather Schuck, author and CEO of Glamajama, has a different view on the subject. She writes, "You will never feel truly satisfied by work until you are satisfied by life."[6] But I most agree with the stance life-transition coach Michael Thomas Sunnarborg takes on the matter: "A true balance between work and life comes with knowing that your life activities are integrated, not separated."[7]

I love work more than most people do, but I think we must be careful in the approach we take to our work. The way I view my life is that I must first live it to the full for my work to be the best that it can be. Work is a byproduct of the life we live; we must not separate the two. As Sunnarborg said, everything in life is integrated. I have previously told people that a work-life balance is achievable, but it only can be because they are one and the same. Life is beautiful in its entirety, including work, but work is to be woven through the fabric of our lives.

There are some seasons where influencing people more means that we put in extra hours and work more, but there are also seasons where people need us to stop. It's each person's responsibility to read the current situation and act accordingly, but it would be irresponsible of me to not communicate how important it is to put in the work, just as long as people don't become workaholics. (I'm not addicted to work, but I am addicted to influence.)

So, rather than asking ourselves, "How do I achieve work-life balance?" a much better question to ask ourselves is, "How can I learn to fall in love with my work and my life?" Because when we find the answer to this question, the only thing we are worried about is having more of what we love, and embracing every opportunity that comes our way—ultimately the fulfillment we were looking for all along in finding the traditional definition of work-life balance. We should be fighting for passion, influence, and impact; not balance.

Of course, you have to figure out what your ideal schedule looks like, but I would challenge you to get to the spot where you are fitting your work around the most important people in your life, rather than the other way around. Society has tricked us for far too long into thinking that work is more important than relationships. But I'm not stupid, and neither are you. No work is worth making our health, our family, our friends, or our other relationships suffer. And if you are unhealthy, you will have nothing to offer to others. It may be time to quit something so you can bring balance back to your life. Take care of your health, and take care of others as well.

### Warning Sign 2: You Are Experiencing Constant Frustration

Frustration alone isn't a reason to quit; it is part of any journey worth taking. In the pursuit of bravery, I can guarantee that you will experience frustration. Don't be afraid of that part. But if the frustration you are experiencing is daily, or even weekly, that's usually a sign that you may need to use your time for something that empowers rather than discourages you.

### Warning Sign 3: You Keep Arriving at Another Dead End

When there's no possible way that you can become better at something, it may be time to move on. If you've already tried studying more to become better, and the people around you aren't making you better, and you honestly can't remember the last thing you learned, then it may be time to quit in order to become better.

A clue that will tell you whether you are currently experiencing a dead end is that the time you've put into doing something is the only reason you keep doing it. When tenure is the sole reason you remain dedicated, it may be time to quit. Also, when something isn't working for an extended period of time, it may be best to just move on. If you have given yourself ample time and you still can't seem to break through, it's probably time to quit.

### Warning Sign 4: Your Plan Isn't Working, No Matter How Hard You Try

Everyone should have a backup plan. As an entrepreneur, I have two businesses and I'm working on a third. Why? Because I have never been one to put all my eggs in one basket. I'm not being pessimistic, but I am being realistic. If we know that bad things can happen, shouldn't we prepare for those things ahead of time? This isn't fear talking; it's realistic preparation.

If you have been following a plan and it isn't working, make a different plan. Maybe the plan looks good on paper, and everyone in your inner circle agrees that it's a great plan, but if it isn't providing the results you want or need, it's time for a new plan.

Many people think their plan A and plan B need to be drastically different, but they don't. Use your previous and present experiences to influence your next plan. It will save both time and energy to build on what you've already accomplished and know. You can use your life experiences to your advantage and construct an even better plan with what you have learned along the way.

### Warning Sign 5: You Would Rather Be Doing Something You Hate

If I feel I would rather be at home doing laundry than doing what I am currently doing, I know that it may be time to quit. Doing laundry is my least favorite thing in the world, so if it sounds more promising than what I'm working on, I force myself to walk away immediately. There's no sense in being miserable; life is way too short for that.

### Warning Sign 6: You Don't Feel Appreciated

If you are living life without feeling loved, it may be time to quit what you are doing and try something different. Of course, I don't mean that you should immediately quit your business or your marriage due to a lack of appreciation, but at the very least, you do need to find a way to work on it and make it better.

Of course, this goes both ways, so if you don't feel appreciated right now, make sure you are doing everything in your power to make those around you feel appreciated as well. Instead of looking at quitting as your first option in this situation, remember that you have the power within you to create a thriving culture of appreciation. If you still don't feel appreciated after you've tried everything you can, it may be time to quit.

### Warning Sign 7: Life Feels Boring or Unsatisfying

There's something to say for living a life full of wonder. Waking up with amazement for each new day is a great way to see the world. When life isn't this way, it is easy to become bored. If you are finding life to be this way, and you've already tried making what you are doing fun, it may be time to quit in order to cultivate a newfound curiosity for the world around you.

### Warning Sign 8: There's Little Value Found in What You Are Doing, Either for Yourself or for Others

When you get to the end of your life, what are you going to want to look back on and find value in? Your answer to this question is what you need to be working on daily. You may need to quit what you are doing in order to find value.

Of course, these are just some indications that it may be time to quit, but knowing what's a good enough reason to quit is half the battle. Quitting is hardly ever the best first solution, but if time goes by and these indicators are still there, it may be time to look at quitting. If quitting immediately sounds too drastic, try this: while contemplating quitting, try other things as you keep attempting to find success in your current endeavors. Testing the waters may provide the answer you are looking for, as it can sometimes offer enough courage to keep you moving ahead, in any direction you choose.

## Change Is Always Good

A defining moment of change in my life happened in my twenties. My wife and I were living in Atlanta, Georgia, at the time, and we sold all of our possessions except what we could fit into our Honda Accord. We embarked on a new adventure, moving to Colorado, without much of a plan, but desperately needing change in our lives. We have since moved to Illinois from Colorado for business, but in that season of life, we needed to prove to ourselves that we could choose bravery over fear. I'm not encouraging you to sell everything you own without much of a plan and move across the country, but if that's what you feel you need, then I would challenge you to at least give it some serious thought.

We intentionally chose this change, because we desperately needed something different, but more often than not, the change that comes will catch you by surprise. While many people don't like the surprise of change, I have grown to love that type of change for the sole reason that it is inevitable. If we know that change is going to take place whether we like it or not, we might as well learn to fall in love with it, right?

If you have ever lost your job, you know that you can look back on that moment and see how it changed your life's trajectory. An event as big as that changes everything. It opens doors for you to pursue something different. It allows you to use what seemed like a scary change to propel you forward. It gives you the opportunity to find something more. Maybe you moved across the country, like we did, just to explore, not really knowing what you were getting into, but you knew that you needed change. Again, this may have brought discomfort, yet you knew it was exactly what you needed. Why? Because change stirs up hope.

The great thing about change is that in most cases it can be as gradual as you want it to be. Sure, there are times in life when change blindsides you, but for the most part, change is rooted in the choices you make along the way.

A great way to adopt change as a positive force in your own life is to pivot. In basketball, pivoting means being able to keep one foot stationary while moving the other foot freely, giving yourself the ability to alter direction as your perception of the court changes. In other words, it gives you the ability to make a needed change, while still holding on to your original reference point. The changes you choose to make in your life can result from pivoting too.

Even if things are terrible, and you feel you need to move to Australia to get away from everything, there's probably no need to change everything in your life right away. I can almost guarantee that there are one or two areas that if attended to could bring just the change you need. You can keep many of your same habits, your same job, and your same environment, while making other changes in your life to give bravery room to happen. Don't think you can't find good in the everyday life you are already living. That would be fear talking again, and the only way to shut its mouth is to stop fearing the effects that change can have on your life. You can be smart with change.

No matter where your journey has taken you, it's time to stop fearing change, because it is one thing in life that will always come. When bad change comes, you can always learn from it. And when good change comes, embrace it for all it offers. For better or for worse, life is full of new passion waiting to be unwrapped. As much as we fear change, we also need—and more than we can fathom—the fresh passion it offers.

But if, for whatever reason, you can't find passion in the midst of change, you can begin by ruling out what you don't like about the change. This can help clarify your vision so you see what other changes need to be made. I am passionate about a lot of things, and if you are like me, you'll find that the passions you need to chase in your own life reveal themselves when you clear away all the things you are not as passionate about. Even in the midst of change, we can all grab hold of passion.

## CHAPTER 8

# The Fear of Losing Control

Once you experience freedom, there's no going back. The need for more freedom in my schedule was the very reason I began pursuing my entrepreneurial dreams in the first place. I was tired of being controlled by my work schedule and needed a more flexible schedule to make room for my family and living a healthier life. Of course, becoming an entrepreneur isn't the answer for everyone, but freedom is. I am convinced that I could never go back to working a fixed schedule, because of my own fear of losing control.

Maybe this scenario sounds familiar, and you are looking to escape from a job that has held you captive for so long. I spent a majority of my life searching for freedom, working away at achieving my ideal life, and wasn't happy until I found what I was looking for. Honestly, I like being in control when I can be, and I do believe that there are key areas of life that we can and should control, like our schedules, our self-perception, and the words we speak. But as good as controlling our lives sounds, there are some things in life that are outside our control. And in this chapter we will look at both.

## Your Words Control Your Freedom

With help from a friend, star hurdler Guy Drut found that he had the power within himself to change his fears. In the summer of 1976, he was the only hope his home country, France, had of winning a medal in track-and-field events at the Summer Olympics in Montreal that year. But the immense pressure to win had bound him up in knots of fear, and he was sure he wouldn't be able to muster the power to pull it off. When one of his friends, Jean-Claude Killy, saw what Drut was going through, he knew how he could help him. Killy's simple advice was to repeat the following words silently to himself over and over again: "I have done everything to get ready for this race, and if I win, everything will be great. But even if I don't win, my friends will still be my friends, my enemies will still be my enemies, and the world will still be the same." Drut agreed to try it, and began repeating this mantra of sorts during all of his practice exercises, breaks, and even in between the semifinal and final qualifying rounds. The advice worked: Drut won the 110-meter hurdles competition and clinched an Olympic victory for France in the 1976 games. Drut says he even kept repeating it when he went up to receive the gold medal![1]

As you can see, the way we handle our fears with our actions and words is within our control. Heeding his friend's advice, Drut finally realized this and saw how his perception of his fear could dictate the outcome of the race positively or negatively, depending on the mindset he chose.

## The Trap of Finding Excuses and Conflict

The most important point in anyone's life is when they finally decide to stop making excuses and blaming everyone else for what is happening and finally take responsibility. Sure, sometimes people are born into bad circumstances, but more often than not the decisions we've made have gotten us where we are.

You may be hurt after feeling disempowered by others, but only in rare instances do you lose your power and control to others. When you feel this has happened, remember that 99 percent of the time you have control over the amount of power you give away. Most people hand their power over to others to avoid conflict. In fact, in my experience, most people have a huge fear of conflict, but the mistake in fearing conflict is to believe that not having conflict is actually healthy. Conflict can solidify a great idea, or it can bring bad ideas to the forefront. Either way, this healthy conflict can only help teams and individuals alike produce better ideas.

To have healthy conflict, you first must learn how to confront other people properly. It's not always about what you want personally, but it is about accomplishing what needs to be done while meeting the needs and interests of everyone involved. Not disagreeing with what you oppose is acting as if everything is perfect when everyone knows that it's not. When we are afraid to communicate, all hope is lost for humanity. Of course, this healthy conflict requires a team of individuals who trusts each other and a belief that everyone involved has the best interests of the entire team in mind. Once teams get to this point, they must begin voicing their opinions and fighting for what they believe to become better. In the end, every opinion is out in the open, and then, narrowing all ideas down to the very best ones produces better teams and better ideas.

While consulting for businesses, I've come across a few that overlooked the importance of conflict, and I've had to show them that civil discourse is what's needed to accomplish more with their teams. I tell you all of this so you realize that against what most people believe to be true, both conflict and compromise are okay. If you've lived life with the approach of "my way or the highway," you probably already know that true freedom will never be found there. You must learn that giving up some control along the way is the beginning of true freedom.

## We Need Compromise and Communication

When did "compromise" become such a bad word? I'll tell you: when people became more concerned with power than with relationships. Power and control are ways to force fear onto others, whereas compromise allows everyone involved to experience bravery. What people don't understand is that trying to control everything in life is a very stressful attempt to fix things that doesn't provide help to anyone else involved. In fact, when people attempt to control things that affect other people, the reaction of others is many times to withdraw from the situation. As much as you want freedom, so do others. As much as you want control, others want some form of control, as well. It's human nature. This is one reason why more flexible hours in the workplace are beginning to be seen as extremely beneficial for employees and businesses alike.[2] People enjoy freedom, but the only way for them to enjoy freedom is for employers to be willing to give up control. That's actually the main reason that giving up control is so important: it give others the opportunity to experience freedom and ultimately live better lives. If you continually attempt to control situations with power in the workplace, people will eventually withdraw; it's only a matter of time. It leaves no other option, because once people taste any sort of freedom found in real relationships and compromise, there's no going back.

Without compromise of any kind, nothing useful happens. However, with compromise, progress is at least made. And with progress, people can begin working toward a brighter future, and that is something everyone should get behind.

Yes, compromise means you have to budge a smidgen on your stance. And, yes, it means you have to hand over some power to another person. Of course, there are some foundational beliefs that people shouldn't compromise on, but what most people miss out on is the fact that compromise leads to a form of agreement in most instances. It can bring people from completely different ends of the spectrum to the middle of the road, allowing them to reach peace. It also opens doors that otherwise would be closed and creates discussion. When compromise isn't an option, and the only option is one person controlling the situation, bridges are burned, not built. Compromise isn't losing but rather mutually sharing power, to come to a better solution.

Combining healthy conflict with compromise is a way for all parties involved to freely communicate their view of the situation. In most situations, communicating without some sort of conflict isn't telling the whole truth. I used to not say how I truly felt in my marriage or as an employee, and then I would get angry that I wasn't getting what I needed. In any relationship, communicating needs to each other is imperative for growth to take place. Both in my marriage and as an employee, the problem was that my expectations didn't match what I was saying. This happened because I wasn't saying anything. Instead of possibly hurting people, I chose to remain quiet, and the problem was that this was more unfair than having healthy conflict. We actually need healthy conflict more than we need peace.

This brings me to my second point. You should never feel bad for communicating what you want. It doesn't mean it will happen, but it is the only way for deep, meaningful relationships to take place. We stop giving control away when we let people know what we want and need to hold on to. This is where compromise can happen. Commit to having healthy conflict and communicate what you need in your relationships both at and outside work, and get much more out of life as a result.

## A Little Solitude Can Sometimes Be Good (But Don't Overdo It)

Writer and critic Marya Mannes said, "The great omission in American life is solitude; not loneliness, for this is an alienation that thrives most in the midst of crowds, but that zone of time and space free from outside pressure which is the incubator of the spirit."[3] And Marya isn't alone in this belief. Sufi poet Rūmī and philosopher Albert Camus also shared a deep devotion to the need for solitude.

As I mentioned earlier in the book, isolating yourself temporarily isn't a bad thing when that solitude will help you move forward in the inspiration part of the bravery process. Research even shows that brainstorming groups think of far fewer ideas than the same number of people who work alone and later pool their ideas.[4] In these times of solitude, ideas come more naturally due to the devotion one gives to the process and the lack of fearing what other people think of one's ideas. Of course, it's important not to get so wrapped up in your alone time that it begins to negatively affect you or those around you. Also, it's impossible to carry out the ideas you've come up with during your solo sessions or use them to positively impact other people's lives if you stay isolated from others. This is why the inspiration stage is the only time in the bravery process when it makes sense to take alone time to brainstorm and dream up ideas (unless alone time is how you recharge, as is true for many introverted people).

Let me give you an example of what I'm trying to say: I place a huge amount of importance on relationships with others. They are what I study, speak, and write about on a regular basis. Why? Because to me, people are the most important thing any of us can affect on this earth. If there's anything to be passionate about, it's helping each other. This is also how we help ourselves.

I love my wife and kids more than anyone else in this entire world, and spending time with my family brings me the utmost joy. I'd love to be with my family 24-7, not only for the special company my wife brings me, but for time to enjoy laughs and piggyback rides with my kids. My daughter and son remind me how quickly time goes—that if I blink, I may miss out on a firefly moment. They give me more purpose, and they remind me how important this journey called life truly is.

So why would I—someone who claims to value relationships, helping others, and being with his wife and family above all—choose to sequester myself from them every so often for short periods of time? Seems counterintuitive, no? Yet forcing myself to spend some time alone now and then actually makes me better. It's how I found the time to write this book, and it's how I initially come up with every idea I have. I've been able to use the inspirations I find while alone to have a positive impact on others, to support those I care about, and hopefully to inspire you to go out and do the same. This is why it is so important to isolate yourself during the idea phase: you can often have your best brainstorms when you are uninterrupted. But we must remember to return to the world once we've finished creating ideas and are ready to act on them, because it is necessary to make time for people as well. When we use our time well, we make passion for our ideas and helping others top priorities.

Often fear rings loudest when we isolate ourselves for too long from others. Actually, this may be the best sign that you have spent too much time in solitude. I've come to realize I can't stay isolated for too long, because I crave connecting with others. I have found that life is a balance of creation and community. This is the balance that helps us push through our fears, and this is what you should strive to achieve. Periods of solitude help push us forward, giving us time to devote to the ideation and creation processes that bring our ideas to life. But it is through building relationships, support networks, and connections with others that we get the fuel to keep the flames of our ideas and inspirations going and growing. Bravery comes forth when you step out of isolation and step into the adventure that relationships are.

## Know When to Step Away . . .

All this sounds great, right? But if you don't have enough time for anything else right now, your best answer is to step away. I know this seems counterintuitive after I just told you to make sure you don't isolate yourself from others too much. But there are times where brief periods of alone time to brainstorm ideas isn't enough to cope with all your daily obligations. Sometimes stepping away to evaluate everything that is happening in your life will help you see the full picture. In the thick of busyness, it is easy to come up with excuses for why we can't make time for being still, but these are the moments when we actually need stillness the most.

So why do I call this practice "stepping away" rather than "taking some alone time or solitude"? Because there will be times, as you're going through the bravery process, when you actually need to physically remove yourself from everything momentarily and look at how far you've come and where you still want to go.

Stepping away is particularly crucial in these chaotic times and in our 24-7 world, because it allows a realignment of priorities to take place. It gives you a new perspective on the world around you, and it helps you appreciate all that you already have.

Whenever you wonder whether it would be a good idea to step away, ask yourself the following questions:

- **Can I become better at what I'm trying to achieve or better as a person by stepping away and reevaluating?**
- **What does stepping away look like for me and what would it take to get me back on track?**
- **How can I be more effective after stepping away for a bit?**

In asking yourself these questions, you may find that stepping away is just the remedy you need to feel free of fear and break out of a rut you've found yourself in.

## . . . And Know When to Commit

The marathon was the final event of the 1968 Olympics in Mexico. The stadium was packed and there was excitement in the air. Way back in the field was a runner named John Stephen Akhwari, of Tanzania. As the race began, Akhwari was eclipsed by all the other runners. After thirty kilometers, his head was throbbing, his muscles were aching, and he fell to the ground. The officials wanted him to retire, but he refused to do so. He was committed to finishing what he had started.

With his knee bandaged, Akhwari picked himself up and hobbled the remaining twelve kilometers to the finish line. All but a few thousand of the crowd had gone home, but that didn't matter. In one of the most heroic efforts of Olympic history, the injured Akhwari finished the race over an hour after the first-place winner completed the race, by collapsing over the finish line. Afterward, when asked by a reporter why he had not dropped out, Akhwari said, "My country did not send me . . . to start the race. They sent me . . . to finish."[5]

As this story shows, not everything in life will go as planned. Sure, you've already read about quitting in a previous chapter, but what about all those times that we are right where we should be, but don't *feel* like pressing forward? This is where commitment fits in.

Like Akhwari, we never have to give in to the temptation to return to safety if we don't want to. It would have been so easy for him to quit after he knew he had already lost, and his body was filled with pain, but he was committed to seeing his efforts all the way to the finish line.

Anyone can live a mediocre lifestyle, because mediocrity is attainable without any effort. Again, in most cases, you don't even choose to be mediocre; it just somehow happens over time. Without a commitment to the journey, luck may happen, but bravery won't. When you commit to your passions, you will begin to see the bravery, and results, you are looking for.

Akhwari was passionate about his craft, and you can pursue passion wholeheartedly, just as he did. While it is always your choice to play it safe or to pursue passion, I implore you to make the best choice right now, which will always include the desire to live out a life full of passion. This desire creates momentum, and if you ever find yourself stuck, it will be the driving force that keeps you fighting fear.

Commitment plays a part in everything you do in life. It requires commitment to finish schooling, it requires commitment to remain married, it requires commitment to build a business and to hold down a job, and it requires commitment to see the biggest return on your investments. Commitment to the right things is a fundamental part of life that results in eventual freedom. No matter what comes your way, know that commitment to putting in the hard work is necessary to find success.

## CHAPTER 9

# The Fear of Being Judged

When life and business coach Marie Forleo was first pursuing her entrepreneurial dreams, she was insecure and embarrassed about what she did for a living. She was pursuing five different passions at the same time, and everything she did confused her friends and family. But the moment she stopped judging herself for being a multipassionate entrepreneur was the moment her passion became clear to others. When she did this, she found herself happy, and that was enough. Her inspiring results can now be seen on her hit weekly web television show, MarieTV, where she shares ideas on creativity, productivity, health and well-being, entrepreneurship, philanthropy, spirituality, and technology. Marie shows us that once we become comfortable with who we are, we become able to fight the fear of being judged, with confidence.[1]

## Confidence

There was a clown at my sixth birthday party. I thought it was great, until the clown had its imaginary dog urinate on my leg. (It was water!) I was mortified in front of all my friends. Looking back at it, I don't really know why I was so embarrassed, but I was. Maybe I didn't know what had just happened, or maybe I didn't understand the joke, but there I was, crying in front of all my friends, not knowing what to do.

There was also the time I met the singer Ciara and said, "I hear people call you Ciara. Well, they call me Adam." I have never heard such a dead silence as the one that followed my lame line. She blinked her eyes four times, I went on my way, and that was the end of our interaction.

And then there was also the time that I was told no when I applied for a promotion within the company that I worked with for ten years. I figured that I was a shoo-in for the job, and it turned out that I wasn't even close. My expectations were too high and I was devastated for months by the bad news.

And last but not least, there was the time that I attempted to raise enough money to build a school in a foreign country, and I didn't gather enough funds. It was my fault because I didn't make the time to put the needed effort into raising the funds, and as a result, I let a lot of people down.

So why do I tell you these stories? Because we've all felt the kind of embarrassment I felt on those days. It stays with us, at the root of our fear of being judged. These are the kinds of moments that keep us humble. Fear will sometimes disguise itself as false humility, but even so, we need to stay humble, my friends. Instead of always trying to impress the individuals around us, what if our actions were based in genuine care? Are you living to impress people, or are you living to help people and add value to their lives? When you pursue the purpose of adding value and helping people, rather than the need to impress people, you will find the confidence to push through any fears that come your way.

I don't care who you are; fear will put a lump in your throat right before you take the first step. I have met a lot of people who want to build a client base for their businesses or an audience for their blogs but don't want to put in the work because they lack confidence. They refuse to market themselves through public speaking or writing because they fear that their words will make them vulnerable.

I feared blogging when I began writing in early 2000, because I was afraid of what readers would say about my work. I feared letting people in and kept what I wrote to myself for a very long time. Not to mention that when I began blogging, there weren't many other people putting their ideas online yet. But I eventually realized that leading requires going first, and any time someone chooses to lead, they must pursue courage above all else.

Feeling vulnerable, or available for attack from others, is the main reason people won't open up in the first place. In a true community, people aren't vulnerable. They're open, because people in a real community aren't out to attack others in their community, but to support them. Choose to embrace your personal story, because that is what makes you unique, and share it within your community. In fact, strive to create community wherever you are, and build confidence in yourself and the people around you while you're at it.

## Introvert, Extrovert, or Ambivert?

Warren Buffett, Bill Gates, Steven Spielberg, Elon Musk, Barack Obama, and Mark Zuckerberg are all introverts, while Tony Robbins, Wayne Dyer, Bill Clinton, Steve Jobs, Richard Branson, Mark Cuban, and Winston Churchill are all extroverts. Personally, I am an ambivert. We are all unique and that is a beautiful thing. Some people are more introverted. They like to keep to themselves, in most instances, and lose energy from being around other people. Then there are extroverts, who are energized by being around other people and talking to them. Extroverts, of course, are more outspoken and tend to rule most conversations. Those of us who don't quite fit into either of these two classic categories are the ambiverts: people who exhibit qualities of both introversion and extroversion.

Some people will give introverts a hard time, because they don't say enough, and some will give extroverts a hard time, because they say too much. But no matter where you fall on the spectrum, don't fall for the lie that says it matters if people judge you for being one or the other. Please don't fear being judged for who you are. You are who you are for a reason, and that's an amazing thing.

But which category you fall into does have a lot to do with how you fight your fears while building relationships. What it doesn't have anything to do with is the common sense and courtesy it takes to listen. It is important not only to focus on what we say and how we say it, but also to focus on listening to the needs of others—introverts, extroverts, and ambiverts alike.

Let's take a moment to look at how listening plays out in the workplace. Studies show that only 12 percent of employees believe that their employers listen to them. 12 percent![2] This has to change.

Listening shows that people are engaged with the world around them, and when individuals have a pulse on what is happening, they can then and only then begin making positive changes.

As you can see, far too often people forget the power found in listening. When people come to talk to you about something, it doesn't mean they always want, or need, your opinion; they may just need you to listen.

Here are three clues to know if you tend to listen first or give your opinion too soon:

## Clue 1: Is Your Immediate Response to Speak or to Listen?

For most of Amgen CEO Kevin Sharer's career, he was an awful listener. His conversations were all about winning arguments and proving that he was smarter than everyone else. But things changed after he heard some life-changing advice from Sam Palmisano. An employee of Kevin's asked Sam in a Q&A session about his business experience in Japan and how it was so successful, and Sam's answer shocked everyone. Sam said that the only reason he was successful in Japan was that he had learned to fully listen to their needs; that's how much of a priority Sam placed on the power found in listening.[3]

Knowing the answer to this question will tell you whether you lean toward giving your opinion first or your first response is to listen to the needs of others. An example of this from my own life was when I had a friend who came to me because he was having trouble in just about every area of his life. He was going through a very rough season and just needed someone to talk to. I was fortunate enough to see this as an opportunity to listen, so I sat there, on the phone, for an hour and fifteen minutes, listening to my friend tell me everything. You know what would have really messed this opportunity up? If I had interjected at some point along the way. The conversation went where it was supposed to go, because I chose to listen. If I had stopped him along the way, I would have been selfishly controlling the conversation and forcing it to go where I wanted it to go. Also, if he was willing to push through his fears and wanted to open up to me, I was going to listen.

But you want to know what happened at the end of the conversation? He asked me what he should do. That's right. I waited my turn. I didn't have to force my opinion on him; he asked for advice when he was ready to hear what I had to say. Too often people interject their own needs into a conversation, without ever considering what the other person needs. Advice given at the wrong time falls on deaf ears, which doesn't help anyone. In most cases, people will ask you for your opinion if they really want it. If they don't ask for it, they will ask someone else, figure it out for themselves, or read advice in a book, or online, from a respected source. Our only responsibility is to be there for others, and many times this comes in the form of listening. The fear of being judged will tell you that you need all the answers, but I promise that you don't need to know everything, nor should you put that sort of pressure on yourself. Just being there for others, in the valleys and on the mountaintops, is enough.

However, speaking does seem to be the main topic of conversation on the subject of communication. I would call myself a writer who speaks, rather than a speaker who writes, but people still come to me for advice on public speaking. Although I haven't had much practice at public speaking lately, because of business and family needs, I do believe it is important for anyone who wants to influence people to develop this craft in one way or another.

I believe people want to get better at public speaking because they think being able to speak in public is the most important form of communication. I do love the fact that public speaking offers a large venue for people to listen to what one has to say, but it is only one form of communication. (I would just invite everyone over for dinner, but my table isn't big enough.) And while I do believe speaking is important, being out in front of people, delivering your opinions, is a very one-sided form of communication. To be a great communicator, you cannot be all talk. At some point you must look at all facets of communication, including the power found in listening.

At the core of this idea is the power found in creating a relationship, and to form a relationship we must focus on both speaking and listening. The trouble with not listening is that people will not want to be around you for long if you never let them get a word in. So if you want to fight the fear of being judged, I would ask, "Have you tried building more relationships with people?" Very rarely is the fear of being judged present in close relationships. Most people feel at risk of being judged by people with whom they aren't closely involved. And if you disagree with me here, I would ask, "Are the people you think you have a close relationship with really that close to you?"

## Clue 2: Do People Come to You for Advice?

If someone has communicated that they are coming to you for advice, then by all means give it. But it is very different if someone is only coming to you to talk. This is where two-way communication and listening to see what the other person needs from you becomes extremely important.

If people repeatedly come to you for advice, it's probably a good sign that you are great at both giving advice and listening. (If you remember, it's also a good sign that you are passionate about the given topic.) You see, these aspects are all connected. One cannot give great advice without first listening to the needs of others. We can all say words without giving them much thought, but it takes a great listener to give passionate, heartfelt advice. That's the mark of someone who loves people and also understands what people need.

### Clue 3: Are You Known as Someone Who Talks Too Much?

About a year ago, I had a phone conversation with a friend of mine that I will never forget. She kept asking questions and wanting me to answer in greater and greater depth. Whatever I said about myself, it wasn't enough, and she would dig deeper. I typically let my work speak for itself and don't care to ramble on about my accomplishments. She finally said, "Adam, you have to learn how to talk about yourself more. People want and need to know more about your work, and you need to give that to them." I simply replied, "I know," and I began talking about something else, to divert attention to a different topic. The truth is that I have never felt very comfortable talking about myself for extended periods of time, as I have always been afraid that it would come off as arrogant or bragging or overconfident.

The phone conversation that day got me thinking about the world as we know it. Everyone is trying to sell something, everyone has something to say, and everyone wants the attention of others. There is much more junk in this world than there are diamonds, or even diamonds in the rough, for that matter, so we are forced to wade through all the junk to find the gems. This being said, it is so important to find your audience for your worthy products and services, so you can begin building trust. And a great way to start building trust and credibility is to first know yourself and then consistently produce great work.

## Know Yourself, Stop Seeking Permission, and Focus on Building Credibility

My favorite quote comes from David Viscott. He said, "The purpose of life is to discover your gift. The work of life is to develop it. The meaning of life is to give your gift away."[4] I know you already have a set idea of who you desperately want to be, but it might not be who you were designed to be; this is why knowing who you really are is so important. When you know who you are, you will finally see where you and your specific gifts fit into the bigger picture.

Choosing to be unique and living a life full of passion will cause you to be misunderstood, but that's okay. Being judged is inevitable when you commit to being yourself, because no one in this world is like you. As much as you want to be accepted by everyone, it will never happen. This is why it is so important to be yourself rather than trying to please everyone, because you will never be able to make everyone happy; you just won't. The people who will love you and/or your work will be there for you, and the ones who don't will still have their opinion no matter how hard you try to please them.

When you're pushing boundaries with your work, there will be many people who don't like it, but that only means that your passion and work aren't for them. That's right—your work isn't for everyone. When you realize that you and/or your work aren't for everyone, it's liberating to say the least.

And seeking approval with your work isn't necessary, because great work produces approval on its own. Terrific results are the easiest way to find your audience and grow it, and nothing shuts critics up faster than producing better results. If people keep criticizing you and your work, don't give them your precious time if you know you're heading in the right direction. Define what success is to you, focus on your work, and fight for success. We all need that from you. Always stay true to who you are and stop asking for permission from others to do what you know you ought to do and you will continually produce the work you were meant to create.

In my own business, the Internet has allowed me to find my audience and influence many people over the years. But what I am most appreciative of is that it has given me a way around seeking permission and approval from others to produce great work. It allowed me to produce work and then find my audience rather than the other way around.

Too many times people ask for permission because they seek inclusion. To seek approval before you begin is to push away any possibility of innovation. Think of anyone who has come before us who had a crazy idea. Do you think that each idea they had or each piece of work was immediately accepted by the masses? It's usually quite the opposite. Anyone who has ever done anything great has had many critics along the way, and it won't be any different for you.

A great example of what I am talking about can be found in the lives of the Wright brothers. The two owned a bicycle repair shop and spent any extra time they had working on their idea of creating a flying machine. They executed their idea over time, made many mistakes along the way to innovation, and eventually created modern aviation on December 17, 1903. Their sense of adventure and innovation showed through their work, but the road to get there was anything but easy. They had their share of people who viewed them negatively along the way, and critics within the European aviation community converted much of the press to an anti–Wright brothers stance. But the Wright brothers kept pressing forward, because they knew who they were, what they wanted to accomplish, and that they were on to something great.[5]

Whether you want to change the aviation business or you have plans to help change a different industry, the principle is the same—even when others don't believe in you, knowing who you are and what you're trying to do will increase belief within yourself, making it much easier to make your ideas a reality.

Steve Jobs with Apple, Phil Knight with Nike, and Howard Schultz with Starbucks—these three businessmen found a gap in the market and filled it with exceptional products. If you research these companies in depth, you will find that they had clarity about their products and who their products were intended for long before they built the companies as you see them today.

On the other hand, some of the world's most unsuccessful brands and businesses have little to no clarity, hoping to appeal to everyone, meaning that they appeal to no one, becoming lost in a sea of competition. This lack of clarity is why half of all businesses fail within the first five years of being open.[6] When you and/or your business don't have a clear picture of where you fit, time is given to things that don't matter; power is given to weaknesses far too often; and the people around you—employees and clients—are left lacking.

When you find your audience and produce work that helps them, credibility will always be the result. Having credibility with people is what extends your reach even further and builds an even bigger audience, meaning that credibility is the foundation for your entire scope of work. Just about the worst thing you could do is to squander opportunities to affect people with important things to say and products that can help them live better lives. The more unimportant information you share, the more noise is added to an already noisy world, and the less long-term attention is earned. (I would say that the only exception is if you're making people laugh—that's important!) Sometimes the bravest thing we can do is to be quiet.

So if we flip the relationship from being a producer to being a member of the audience, how can we help others with the fear of being judged? We can all start with viewing people who share information with us online as individuals who are trying to build credibility, not as people who are only trying to sell us something. This means you must begin seeing the good in people far in advance of focusing on the bad in them.

On the other hand, if people don't believe in you, they will never be able to believe in your message. For people to follow, they must know that they can trust you, and to do so they need to know who you truly are. People need all aspects for you, both the good and the bad, to begin building credibility through a relationship with them.

So here are five specific areas to focus on to produce more credibility in your own life:

- **Character matters.** Instead of thinking about what so-and-so would do, think about what the right thing to do is. If you are the same person behind the scenes as you are in front of people, then you eliminate the fear of people finding out about the real you.
- **Realize that you don't know everything.** In doing this, you will find what you do know and focus on those things—not to mention the fact that humility is an important trait to possess in itself. Doing this will increase your expertise in your specific field of study or work.
- **Overdeliver!** Nothing produces credibility like going the extra mile.
- **Be who you are.** There are enough copycats out there, so stop trying to be like everyone else.
- **Be honest.**

In following these steps, you will produce credibility and will ultimately communicate the things with your life that you want people to receive from you.

## The #1 Way That People Feel Judged

I have talked to hundreds of people about their fears, and I have found one constant truth when it comes to the fear of being judged. People feel judged when they fear an area of their life disqualifies them from doing what they want to do. So what's the biggest area of perceived disqualification, you ask? Age. In many cases, people feel they only have ten to fifteen years to contribute their full selves to the world, that during all the other years they are either too young or too old to make a difference. Well, I couldn't disagree more. If you have been sold the idea that you are too young or too old to be successful, you need to change that mind-set. If you are able to jump into your desired role early on in life, you will only become better and better over time. And if you're jumping late, you're bringing along the wisdom and experience of all your years.

When people are able to jump the mental hurdle of age, results and opportunities skyrocket. When you don't allow boundaries to keep you from reaching your dreams, anything is possible. Life is more about the power of the ideas at hand, paired with passion, determination, and hard work. These are the things that matter most in the pursuit of bravery, not age.

The first person who comes to mind is Facebook CEO Mark Zuckerberg. At age twenty-nine, he didn't see his age as an obstacle to starting Facebook, but instead saw an opportunity to use his passion. Keith Cozza was able to see past his age, as well. At age thirty-five, Cozza is the CEO of Icahn Enterprises. Thirty-three-year-old Daniel Schwartz, CEO of Burger King, and thirty-five-year-old Robert J. Pera, CEO of Ubiquiti Networks, didn't see their ages as obstacles either. All these people saw their chance, were able to fight fear, and found success in their passion: running a business. Of course, these are only a few people who decided to overlook their age and to step out to do something because they believed in their idea enough to make it happen. If you feel too young to find bravery, then what you want to happen will not happen until you fight your fear of being judged.

Maybe you are on the other side of this mentality. Maybe you have already gone through the "I am too young" mentality, have already put your time in, and have found yourself in another waiting season that you didn't see coming. Maybe you are at the point of feeling that you are too old to provide anything of worth and feel that you are better off keeping to yourself, in retirement? Or maybe you are near retirement and feel that it is better for you to keep your head down and provide just enough to stay in your job until your time is up?

Fear says a lot of things, but the fear that rings loudest for many people is "it's too late." Whether you are late in your years and want to start a business (Harland David Sanders franchised his first Kentucky Fried Chicken when he was sixty-two, Charles Flint was sixty-one when he launched IBM, and Anita Crook was fifty-nine when she started her handbag organizer business called Pouchee) or you are older and want to impact people in a different way, know that it's never too late to chase your ideas. If you are middle-aged or older, and feel it is too late to start over, remember that the next fifteen years are more important than the last fifteen years. You have so much to give with your life, no matter where you are in your journey. And you can start moving now.

## CHAPTER 10

# The Fear of Something Bad Happening

When I was four, my sister broke my leg in a pillow fight. (You can laugh.) I saw her about to hit me with her pillow, so I did what I thought I should do: I put my leg through a rocking chair to brace myself for impact. Smart, huh? For some reason I thought this was a good idea, but as her pillow hit me, my body stayed in one place and my leg went another direction. I ended up breaking my leg in four places, and for months I was in a cast from hip to toe.

Just as I braced for impact in that crazy pillow fight, the world seems to be bracing, right now, for something terrible to happen. The imminent threat of countries going to war with one another and worldwide government and business debt spinning out of control all leave us thinking about what tragedy could possibly happen next. But as long as we are preparing for the worst and hoping for the very best, while not fearing a terrible outcome, we are doing exactly what we should be doing to find bravery.

## The Reality of Tragedy

Yes, as much as I speak and write about the positive side of life, tragedy will come at some point. I think of three friends of mine who have recently experienced tragic events. Not long ago someone in my online community had their seven-year-old son pass away from brain cancer. I also went to a funeral for my close friend's eleven-year-old boy. And just a few months before that, another good friend's little boy passed away. These are heavy events to deal with, but reality tells me that tragedy happens, no matter how much we try to avoid it.

Many times in life I have intentionally sheltered myself from tragedies like these; such moments can almost be too heavy to deal with. As you know, joyous times are much easier to celebrate. You will never get to the end of your life and say, "You know, I wish I hadn't been so happy. It was such a waste." But the reality is that we are given relationships for the opportunity to travel alongside friends, both to the mountaintops and down into the valleys of tragedy. This applies to every relationship you build along the way, including the benefit of having other people in your own life. People will have the opportunity to travel mountaintops and valleys with you, as well.

Things will come into your life that you never planned for, whether tragic events in your personal life, as for my friends, or in your business. But there's hope. I looked on from the outside during all three of these terrible situations to see how my friends handled their tragedies, and I was amazed at the grace they were able to find in the midst of pain. When my friends lost their children, when others I know lost all their money in their business ventures, and others lost their jobs, I've seen that they all somehow found bravery.

So, what's the difference between the people who keep fighting their fears and those who lose all hope? There are a few factors, but the individuals who keep fighting are above all characterized by an unbridled determination in the midst of tragedy. They see that beauty can always be found, no matter what happens, and are able to optimistically continue pressing forward. Yes, tragedy comes, and nothing I say will ever diminish its magnitude, but even more powerful is the experience of restoration—the mountaintop after the experience of tragedy. If you are in the midst of tragedy, remember that restoration will eventually come. The anxiety that comes from worry doesn't bring success into your life any faster. Fear be still, bravery come near.

## How to Prepare for Inevitable Difficult Times

Sir John Franklin set sail in 1845 to chart the Northwest Passage through the Canadian Arctic to the Pacific Ocean. For a voyage that was to last two to three years, the crew packed only their uniforms, and the captain carried only a twelve-day supply of coal for the two ships' auxiliary steam engines. As soon as the ships sailed into frigid, ice-filled waters, it became very clear that the entire crew was in much more trouble than they had prepared for. Ice coated the decks, the spars, and the rigging. Then water froze around the rudders, and the ships became hopelessly trapped in the frozen sea. Sailors set out to search for help but soon succumbed to the severe Arctic weather and died of exposure to harsh winds and subfreezing temperatures. None of the 138 men aboard returned. They had prepared as if they were embarking on a short cruise, rather than on a grueling voyage through one of earth's most hostile environments.[1]

This story shows what happens when we don't prepare. When our expectations don't meet our reality, we let fear and disaster have the upper hand. When we don't prepare, there is no possible way that we can give our journey our all.

Merriam-Webster defines "preparation" as "the action or process of making something ready for use." If more people actually knew what they were doing before they embarked on a journey, fewer bad things would happen. Of course, you don't need to know everything before you begin, because that would be nonsense. Many times, the best way to learn is from hands-on experience, which can only happen in experimentation and putting in the actual work.

You will always learn more than you expect in the course of the bravery process. But preparation indicates that you care enough to devote your time and passion to something worth pursuing. Preparation is what qualifies you for an even bigger future. Prepare now, and use what you have learned from your experiences in the future.

That said, my advice will never be "just go do it," when no preparation has been put into the "it." That's awful advice. We have brains and the ability to conduct research for a reason.

Research is necessary to become the person you want to be. When I was trying to figure out the schedule that would work for me, it took a lot of time and effort on my part to find it. After much trial and error, I reached out to fifty other entrepreneurs through e-mail to see what worked for them. I found that where my schedule was out of whack, these individuals seemed to have it all figured out. I actually contribute much of my productivity levels to this process of research, and you can experience the same benefits in your area of research.

Are you having trouble in the area of relationships? Find someone who is great at developing meaningful relationships and start asking questions. Do you have more unanswered leadership questions than you have answers? Find someone who you would consider to be a great leader and begin asking them questions. Do you need to become a better communicator? Find a great communicator and begin asking questions. Do you need to become more focused? Find someone who gets more done in their day than most do in a week and start asking questions. Do you need more creativity in your life? Find someone who oozes creativity and begin asking them questions. Whatever area you need help in, there are people who want to help you become better. There are people who are available and willing to listen. It amazes me how easy a concept this is, and yet people miss out on it time and time again.

We need to conduct more research and ask more questions, because it is the practice of asking better questions that reveals better answers. When you know what other successful people do, you can emulate their actions in your own life and reap the benefits for yourself. This allows you to skip over unnecessary trial and error, and gives you more time to live a better life.

One of the best ways to know if you are making a good decision or not is to look at others who made the same decision in a past similar situation, and decide if they experienced an outcome that you want to experience for yourself. The results may not turn out the exact same way, but they will most likely be close. The past is full of data that's there to learn from, not to ignore.

And speaking of data, Google is known as one of the most data-driven companies in the world. They collect it, analyze it, and make better decisions due to being aware of the past decisions that their users have made. They use detailed data to their advantage, and you should do the same. Making this small tweak to your decision making process will save you from having many headaches along the way and will only ensure a better success rate with your decisions. Seek to understand, take notes on your findings from research, analyze the data, implement what works in your own life, learn from mentors, and do your best work.

While everything in life is a process, and there is no better time to begin than now, you shouldn't be taking one giant leap to your end goal. Baby steps, baby steps, my friend. Dedication to your journey, paired with the perseverance to push through difficulty along the way, is what makes you stronger and wiser.

If the answer were to just go do it, you wouldn't be dealing with your fear of bad things happening. Yes, moving away from playing it safe is the first step—once you have your great idea. And doing things even when you are afraid is what separates those who find bravery from those who let safety win out. But your first focus should be finding an idea worth looking past your fear for.

When people shoot for the stars without first building a rocket, they unnecessarily set themselves up to lose hope. To hit a bull's-eye, people need tools and training. What tools do you need to succeed? What training do you need to succeed? The answers to these two questions will show you what you need to begin the best possible practices right now. Then, once you are prepared, trial and error will lead to bravery.

If you've prepared and still find that something isn't working, it's probably because you missed a step along the way. Here it is important to take time to evaluate the situation at hand before you continue to move forward. The advice to "just do it" makes you expect to have your dreams right away, but life just doesn't work that way. Honestly, the process is the most enjoyable part. It's where you make mistakes. It's where you learn from the mess that life is. It's where you affect people along the way. And it's where you realize just how far you've come. The journey is necessary to prepare you for an even brighter future. The question is, are you willing to put in the time and work?

## Build Security for the Future

Daymond John founded the company FUBU and is an investor on the hit TV show *Shark Tank*. What I love about John's journey is that even after he started FUBU, and the business was beginning to grow, he held down a day job at Red Lobster, to make ends meet, without sacrificing his business. As a CEO, he used to his advantage the flexible hours that the other job offered. The fact that he could leave his work at work every day and spend a majority of his time working on FUBU between shifts was a huge benefit.[2]

I followed John's model and built my business while owning another, more secure, business to bring in income. I did this because I was afraid that my business wouldn't grow and we would end up living on the streets. While this may have been extreme, that mental picture got me to focus on my work like I never had before. I worked day and night so my business would succeed. My fear that motivated me to put more effort into business paid off. Fear became my motivation, and if all else fails, you can use fear to your advantage too.

Many times we know what is best for us, even in the midst of fear, yet we do something else. This is called lack of self-discipline. When we know we need to fight fear, and don't, we are not giving our psyche what it needs to survive. Sure, fighting fear is a lot of work, but living a life that is full of success is a lot of work too. People need to stop trying to escape their fears, and instead fight them, because the time and effort we put in fighting our fears can strengthen our desire to see success.

## Managing Stress Levels

It may take a few more years to see your dreams come true, so there is no need to put any part of your life in jeopardy. What you need is more patience, not high levels of stress. Maybe you have lost sight of the need to enjoy life while on the journey, but there's a fix for that. Remembering that everything you do now is building security for the future is what will keep you grounded. When people lose sight of this truth, the road to their dreams becomes miserable, not enjoyable. And if you can't enjoy the pursuit of the things that you want most out of life, then what can you enjoy? Speaking of living an enjoyable life, I once heard a story that explains how the stress we encounter works, and it fits nicely here:

> A lecturer explaining stress management to a class raised a glass and asked, "How heavy is this glass of water?" The answers called out ranged from twenty to five hundred grams. The lecturer replied, "The absolute weight doesn't matter. It depends on how long you try to hold it.
>
> "If you hold it for a minute, that's not a problem. If you hold it for an hour, you'll have an ache in your right arm. If you hold it for a day, you'll have to call an ambulance. In each case, it's the same weight, but the longer you hold it, the heavier it becomes." He continued, "And that's the way it is with stress. If we carry our burdens all the time, sooner or later, as the burden becomes increasingly heavy, we won't be able to carry on. As with the glass of water, you have to put it down for a while and rest before holding it again. When we're refreshed, we can carry on with the demands of life."

We have all dealt with stress and can see the truth in this story. In fact, 44 percent of Americans feel more stressed than they did five years ago. One in five Americans experience extreme stress, including shaking, heart palpitations, and depression. Work stress causes 10 percent of strokes. Stress is the basic cause of 60 percent of all human illness and disease. And three out of four doctor's visits are for stress-related ailments. Talk about the fear of something bad happening! As you can see, stress is a big deal.[3]

To know how to handle the stress that comes from our fears, we must look at the opposite of stress, which is peace. Peaceful people tend to put themselves in less stressful situations. People who are peaceful avoid comparing themselves to other people, keep their schedules open, and are able to remain present rather than thinking about the next thing they have to do. In other words, they find ways to reduce or eliminate unnecessary stresses. Some people enjoy wearing busyness as a badge of honor, but it is only when we stop doing this that stress can be reduced.

Think of how much better life would be if you were able to eliminate some of the stress you experience. You would be ecstatic if you could do this, right? But sometimes it is easier said than done.

If you are having trouble reducing stress in your life, here are eleven things you can try right now:

- **Sleep more**
- **Reframe problems**
- **Have realistic expectations**
- **Work to change your worldview**
- **Forgive the people you need to forgive**
- **Laugh every single day**
- **Learn to say "I'm sorry" when you need to and to move on**

- **Procrastinate less**
- **Keep a journal**
- **Have a creative outlet**
- **Volunteer your time**

Yes, stress will come, but it is our job to let it go quickly. The more often we strive for peace rather than give in to fear, the less stress we will feel. And how do we fight fear? The answer will always be passion. If your biggest fear is that something bad will happen, know that an even more important fear is that you haven't done something with your life. And the only way to do something with your life is to take the first step with your amazing ideas.

## Stop Waiting to Be Chosen—Choose Yourself!

Remember what it felt like waiting to be picked for a dodgeball or basketball team in gym class? Somehow I always managed to be picked in the middle of the pack. Not first, not last, but right in the middle. Still, the wait was always agonizing, because, like everyone else, I never wanted to be picked last.

Of course, this scenario probably looked very different for anyone who was really athletic. They were always fought over, as everyone wanted to pick them first. I sometimes wonder what happened to all those people who were picked first. Did they keep being "picked first," even well into their careers, and go on to be successful *because* they were given this boost of confidence early on by their peers? And what about the people who were picked last? Are they still being picked last today, or did they use that as an impetus to prove their skills and abilities in other areas?

You see, I've always disliked having to be chosen to be able to do something. I didn't like having to be picked to be on someone's team—why couldn't I simply join the team and contribute however I could? But the good news is that if you don't want to wait to be picked for someone's team, or to find out you haven't been chosen, you can find or create a new game. If you don't want to be picked for a job, you can always start a new business. There's always a way around being picked.

Now, I'm not saying that we can all do whatever we please, whenever we please. That wouldn't work either, and there are many benefits to being part of a team, one being that you get to learn how to get along with everyone. I am just saying that many of the world's most successful people didn't wait to be picked, but instead they picked themselves. No, it won't be an easy journey, but you already have the passion you need to be a success. It's time to pick yourself.

## CHAPTER 11

# The Fear of Getting Hurt

Every Tuesday, I meet with a group of people who get together from completely different walks of life. We have a meal together and talk about what is happening in our lives. It's a great idea, because otherwise I would never carve out time for a meal with twelve other people on a weekly basis. At first everyone was afraid of opening up to complete strangers, but after our first night together, we became much more comfortable with one another. How did this happen? I asked each person to tell their story.

The best way to fight the fear of getting hurt is to do life together and to get to know one another on deeper levels. Some will argue that building close relationships with others can only leave you hurt in the end, but living life without relationships sounds much more hurtful than never experiencing the beauty found in relationships. So I started by telling my story and encouraged others to join in the fun.

We've all been hurt in some way, but telling people our stories helps us all relate to one another and opens the door for everyone to share their stories too.

Looking at this group now, months after we met for the first time, I see that we are truly passionate about one another's needs. In fact, I can't imagine life without them. We all care about the wants and needs of each member of the little community we've created, and we passionately want to see one another succeed. We no longer fear that we will be hurt by someone in the group putting us down, because trust has been built. It has taken some time, but we have progressed from being strangers to becoming friends. Relationships give us the opportunity to be brave, and we must not squander these valuable moments. We now all feel safe, and it began with saying something personal about ourselves and listening to where each person had come from.

People often don't get close to others because they are afraid of getting hurt. But with anything in life, there is always a chance that it will end badly. The fear of getting hurt is linked to the bad consequences we may encounter. If we make the consequences of everything we may do wrong in life bigger than our passion for what's right, the fear of getting hurt wins out. In the case of our weekly group, we let the compassion and love in our hearts win out.

Fear of getting hurt in relationships keeps walls up, and openness is what tears walls down. So when something terrible comes your way, remember that it is just another chapter in your book that you will share with others in the future. It is a small part of what makes you who you are, and brings you another step closer to bravery.

Suzanne Styles understands this idea. She experienced a catastrophic business failure in late 2011, and little did she know the impact it was going to have on every part of her life. She lost her home, her car, her paintings, her jewelry, and, more devastatingly, she lost her family, her children, and just about all her friends. As a result of the shame from this experience, her self-confidence and self-esteem diminished. But after three-and-a-half years of being crippled by shame, she finally realized that she had to take control. She began sharing her story with others, and her pain helped others gain control of their own lives. Her hurt actually helped others who were going through similar experiences.[1]

Even if your story is painful like Suzanne's, the pain you experience will always hold valuable lessons. Pain reminds us of consequences, pain leaves a lasting reminder to not waste a minute, and pain changes your outlook on the world if you allow it to. Even though pain will always be found in love, one cannot be brave without extending passion toward another person.

## Love and Passion Work Together

Love and passion work together because they are the only two forces that are more powerful than fear. When you have passion for something, or someone, your need for bravery becomes bigger than yourself. Passion is the fire that burns in your being and longs to be released; passion is the substance that motivates your pursuits; passion is what causes you to move; and passion can even affect your outlook on life. You can direct that same passion into the ideas you can't shake, so you are compelled to take action on them. Become submerged in your passion for this world, and do everything in your power to draw out your best ideas.

When passion is there but isn't sought after, we settle for complacency. And it is this complacency that leads to giving up on the best plans for our lives. I don't know about you, but to me that sounds deeply depressing. Don't fall for the lie that you can't pursue passion because you may be hurt somehow. And don't say that passion isn't reason enough to follow something. If this is true, what is a good enough reason to find bravery? Money? Fame? Stability? If you don't find passion and ultimately bravery, life becomes a game in which you are continually waiting for luck to show up. Is that what life was meant to be? I sure hope not. I didn't sign up for living a life like that, and I know you didn't either.

Bravery is a trial-and-error experiment that everyone must partake in, because only you know the risks that you are willing to take. Maybe you find yourself waiting for the next big thing to just somehow happen. You are hoping doors will open at just the right moment. But that's not how things happen. You will find more long-term hurt in playing it safe than you ever will in pursuing your dreams—I can promise that.

In fact, some of the worst advice I've ever received is to wait as long as you need to for doors to open. I found bravery, not by taking slammed doors in my face as a sign to give up, but by using passion as a crowbar to pry doors open. If an open door means that it is "meant to be," and a closed door means that it "isn't meant to be," you are robbing yourself of the opportunity to fight with passion and bravery for what you believe in. I wish I could give you a magic formula that would tell you whether you should try to force your way into something or not, but again, bravery is more about passion and using trial and error to your advantage than anything else. Take some chances, make some mistakes, and if nothing works, remember that the past is always there to learn from.

## Look to the Past for Clues to the Future

I have to force myself to analyze my past. Why? Because it's necessary. Of course we don't want to dwell negatively on our past, because we can't change what has already been done, but we can continually learn from our past and change our lives for the better with this one simple practice.

There are three main reasons I believe looking at your past is one of the most important things you can do to fight the fear of getting hurt:

### Reason 1: Looking at Your Past Helps Ensure That Bad
####      History Doesn't Repeat Itself

We've all had times in life that didn't turn out so well, but we can turn those hurtful experiences into positive ones by not being afraid to look at them. Although it may be uncomfortable, we can work to not only look at the past but learn from it. Science historian James Burke said, "Why should we look to the past in order to prepare for the future? Because there is nowhere else to look."[2] We should look at our past mistakes and victories and take advantage of them, for the sole reason that we can.

The only way to know that bad history won't repeat itself is to make changes so the future won't turn out the same way. Want to change your future? Understand what you want to be known for and begin building your life around those things. You can begin making braver choices right now.

### Reason 2: Remembering What Has Happened Before Gives You Incredible Stories and Lessons to Share with Others

Not only does looking at your past improve your memory, but making this a regular practice helps you to never forget where you came from. Some of the best stories I share now are from the distant past. This is fun for me, because I can see each obstacle I have overcome to get where I am today. You've done the same thing in your own life, and it's these experiences that make you who you are.

Every time you don't make use of your past in some way, you rob others of experiences you have already encountered. You already have valuable insight into situations that others may encounter in their journeys, so you might as well begin using your past for good. You can share your past to help someone else's future.

### Reason 3: Reexamining Your Past Can Show You What You Can Improve

Looking at your past tells you if you have been working in your strengths or weaknesses. Looking at the past will also tell you if you have been working toward bravery in your ideas. Based on this analysis you will have a good idea of what kind of improvements need to be made. If you have been working toward bravery with your ideas, then that's amazing. Keep it up! But if you've been heading in the opposite direction, then by all means make the needed improvements now instead of "someday." Make looking at your past a habitual practice. It will not only help you now but will assist you in making improvements for the future.

## The Value of Regret—and of Letting Go

We've all experienced regret at some point in our lifetime, and Billy Crystal is no different. As you probably know, Crystal has starred in movies such as *City Slickers*, *When Harry Met Sally*, *The Princess Bride*, *Monsters, Inc.*, and many others. In his illustrious career, he only has one regret—saying no to playing Buzz Lightyear in *Toy Story*. Crystal admitted, "It's the only regret I have in the business of something I passed on."

The regret he talks about is just another part of life when trying different things. He turned down that role to focus on what he considered to be better opportunities. Does he need the role of Buzz Lightyear to make his career better? I would argue that he doesn't, not to mention that his voice probably wouldn't even have been a good match. (I need to add "movie critic" to my bio.) Crystal may fear that he missed out on an opportunity, but the rest of us don't see it that way.[3]

The one negative that can come from looking at the past for too long is the "should've, would've, could've" game, which always leads to regret. Regret comes when you are unable to see all you have and focus instead on all you don't have. So if you're among the 90 percent of people who say they have a major regret, the key is to learn from regret and keep moving toward bravery.[4]

What most people don't realize, however, is that regret is part of bravery. When you test the waters to see if you will sink or swim, there will be some regret along the way. Living a life without regret is boring, and it's a complete myth that you can avoid regrets while taking bold moves. When you finally accept that regret is just another part of life, you will see that there's no need to beat yourself up over missed attempts.

Perhaps you have only chased an idea once or twice in your lifetime, but you probably already know that as you pursue bravery more often than not there will be things that you wish you could take back. When these moments come, it is up to you to turn regrets into scenic detours and mistakes into glorious triumphs. Live life to the full, marked with regret from taking chances that didn't pan out, so that when you look back you know you gave life your all. Today you have the opportunity to shape your future with passion, and in doing so bravery will make you into someone amazing, regret and all.

While pursuing bravery will leave you with regrets, never fighting fear will leave you with more regret than making mistakes along the way ever could. Actually, never finding bravery will leave you with more regret than anything you will ever encounter, so go try something new, and learn some valuable lessons from living life with passion.

I would rather live life regretting that something didn't quite end up how I wanted it to, instead of living life with the regret of never trying at all. Refusing to be brave isn't living—it's called hiding. Never allow regret to keep you from bravery, because when you begin seeing regret for what it truly is, bravery is much closer than you think.

## The Problem with Insecurity

Maybe this is the first time someone has told you to view regret in this light. Maybe regret has caused you to be insecure about yourself and what to do next. Insecurity either breeds a larger-than-life ego, and pride that tends to put other people down along the way, or it leaves you unable to voice your opinion.

The number one thing that causes people to shy away and propels insecurity is public or peer-to-peer humiliation, and it is something I have vowed to stand against. If I see someone else being humiliated, I will do everything in my power to take care of it, no question, whether it involves me or not. When a culture of humiliation is present, positive growth and individual freedoms are suppressed, which is damaging to all of us. If you are being humiliated or you see others who are being humiliated, or harassed, be brave and don't allow it. You have the right and responsibility to speak up.

One way people can protect themselves from humiliation is to surround themselves with only those who agree with them. But that's never the best way to fight the fear of getting hurt. When people don't agree with us, it forces us to look at things from other perspectives, not just our own. It forces us to relinquish our complacent "right" not to analyze reality. Even if you don't want to see it, others will help you see what's really going on. When people only tell you what you want to hear, the facts disappear, and along with them the opportunity to make things right.

If you are currently dealing with insecurity, you need to ask yourself, "Is my insecurity more important than making a huge difference in this world?" Even though passion is the missing link in many bravery equations, the answer to this question shows why passion will help you find your bravest self. Passion for something will tell you that you need to move toward it, because if you don't, you will suffer.

To build confidence in the midst of insecurity, you can begin focusing on both your strengths and weaknesses right now. Confidence is situational for most people, depending on whether or not they feel talented in a specific area. I am guessing that the things you feel less confident about are the same things you consider to be your weaknesses. This is only natural. I know that I talk a lot about the need for people to find their strengths and to work within them, but that's only half of the story. For you to believe in the "only follow your strengths" mentality is to say that some areas of life don't matter, and we both know that isn't true. Working on your weaknesses allows you to become your bravest self.

If you are experiencing insecurity, and have believed the lie that you are not good enough for something or someone, know that you are good enough. At some point you have believed the lie that you need to impress others, but more than anything else, you need to be you, because that's the only thing that will help change the world for the better.

## Remember: You Are Valuable

I find art fascinating. For something to be created, an artist must first think up an incredible idea, or see something so beautiful that it inspires them to create, and then have enough passion to begin and complete a work of art. It truly is a beautiful thing to behold.

One interesting thing about art is how its worth is evaluated. The rarity of the art, its role in breaking new ground, how it's interpreted, and who painted it all play a part in the overall value of a piece. If a painting is one of a kind, and it speaks to people, and the artist who painted it is famous, then the painting will sell for a high dollar amount.

Now, let's apply this principle to your own life. You are one of a kind. There is no one else in this world like you, and you have the ability to break new ground with bravery every single day. In other words, you are priceless, and your life can speak value into the lives of others.

Know that what you do matters, because you are valuable. You are here on this earth for a reason. To live with passion, to look for answers, to passionately love—life is a beautiful opportunity to impact the world in magnificent ways.

But even in all of this there will be people who don't like you, people who you won't get along with, people who won't accept you, and people who don't care for your work. Such is life. If you understand these things, it is much easier to see your own value when life doesn't go as planned. In the end, the only worthy reason to continue fighting your fears is the people around you. Make people your passion, and find the reason behind the reason to do everything you do. This is the secret in finding passion and fighting your fears. Other people always make the bravery journey worth the effort.

## A Final Word

My first hope is that reading these eleven chapters was life-changing for you. (Or that at least some parts of them were!) And if we were sitting down over coffee and you asked me my thoughts on fear, this is exactly what I would tell you. (I can be a little long-winded sometimes, so I thank you for bearing with me and hope it was worth the effort.) But all of these words don't mean a thing if you don't do anything with them. The usefulness of everything in this book becomes contingent on your action. So my second hope is that these words stir something new inside of you. A new voice, a new passion for life, a newfound courage, a new determination to succeed—or at the very least to try. Because fear is the number one obstacle you will face in life: the most difficult challenge you will ever be put to and the most important one to overcome. But I have no fear and no doubt that you can do it. And the best part is that you now have everything you need to be the bravest you.

## ACKNOWLEDGMENTS

First, I want to thank God, because without him, I'd be lost on this grand adventure called life. I want to thank my wife, Jasmine, for picking me. You saw potential in me before I saw potential in myself, and for that I am beside myself. The love you have for our family is absolutely beautiful. Thank you to my precious daughter, Colbie. I'll never forget the moment you made me a dad. Your bravery is contagious, and I can't wait to see what you do with your superpowers. Thank you to my two-year-old son, Nolan. You already inspire me to be a better person, and I can't wait to see the man you become.

Mom, thank you for showing the rest of us how to love others. Your tenacity keeps me in awe. Thank you, Dad, because without you I wouldn't be where I am today. Your hard work has always inspired me to do more with my life. Sarah, thank you for being a wonderful sister. You're one of the smartest people I know, and that has always given me something to strive for. Thank you, Crawford, for being an amazing brother. I can't wait to see what you do next.

Thank you to the Rasmussens and the Sanders. My family and I are eternally grateful for your friendship. Thank you Kip, Andy, Arden, Ben, Beth, Bob, Bridget, Claudia, Curt, Darin, Denice, Jacob, Jadyn, James, Jami, Jason, Jimmy, Josh, Karen, Maria, Miriam Ruth Thompson, Miriam Rebekah Thompson, Tony, and Yasmin for your encouragement and kindness.

I want to thank my staff for making sure my businesses don't miss a beat. Thank you, Glenn, for inspiring me and everyone else to become better leaders. Thank you Andre, Christina, Courtney, Daniel, Dewitt, Erik, Jackie, Jacob, Jed, Jordan, Julia, Kirby, Leo, Nate, Reade, Ryan, and Vincent for providing years' worth of content. Thank you to Larry at Oqobo for making everything work. Thank you to my online community and customers who have been there for me for the past ten years. You all made this book possible.

Thank you to my agent, Jim Hart, who championed my work from my very first manuscript. Thank you to my editor, Stephanie Bowen, for believing in this message. Your bravery made this book a reality. Thank you to Jessica Morphew and the Art Department at TarcherPerigee for a perfect book cover. Thank you to Joel Fotinos and the rest of the team at TarcherPerigee for getting these words into people's hands. Working with Penguin Random House on this book has been a pleasure.

And thank you to everyone else who has made me laugh, taught me something useful, or encouraged me along the way. Your positivity has made me a better person.

# NOTES

## CHAPTER 1

1   Harvey Mackay, "Success Can Breed Complacency," *Times Union*, January 26, 2015, http://www.timesunion.com/tuplus-business/article/Harvey-Mackay-Success-can-breed-complacency-6041570.php.

2   Emily Co, "What a Mayonnaise Jar Can Teach Us About Life," POPSUGAR Smart Living, March 21, 2016, http://www.popsugar.com/smart-living/Mayonnaise-Jar-Two-Cups-Coffee-Story-34745305.

3   Steven Bertoni, "Start-up 'Hello' Goes from Kickstarter to Target and Best Buy in Less Than 2 Years," *Forbes*, November 1, 2016, http://www.forbes.com/sites/stevenbertoni/2016/11/01/start-up-hello-goes-from-kickstarter-to-target-and-best-buy-in-less-than-2-years/#584bec3f7682.

4   Gail Matthews, "Goals Research Summary," Dominican University of California, 2015, http://www.dominican.edu/academics/ahss/undergraduate-programs/psych/faculty/assets-gail-matthews/researchsummary2.pdf.

5   Miller Center of Public Affairs, University of Virginia, "Franklin D. Roosevelt: Life in Brief," http://millercenter.org/president/biography/fdroosevelt-life-in-brief.

6    M. K. Suvak and L. F. Barrett (2011). "Considering PTSD from the Perspective of Brain Processes: A Psychological Construction Approach," *Journal of Traumatic Stress* 24(1), 3–24, http://www .ncbi.nlm.nih.gov/pmc/articles/PMC3141586/.

7    B. Kulkarni, D. E. Bentley, R. Elliott, et al. (2007). "Arthritic Pain Is Processed in Brain Areas Concerned with Emotions and Fear," *Arthritis & Rheumatology* 56(4), 1345–54, http://onlinelibrary.wiley .com/doi/10.1002/art.22460/full.

8    Robert L. Leahy, *The Worry Cure* (New York: Harmony Books, 2005).

9    Statistic Brain Research Institute, "Fear/Phobia Statistics," 2016, http://www.statisticbrain.com/fear-phobia-statistics/.

10   Lewis Howes, "No More Excuses" (podcast), http://lewishowes .com/podcast/no-more-excuses/.

11   Lawrence Block, *Telling Lies for Fun & Profit* (New York: Quill, 1994).

12   Scott Davis, "Broncos Superstar Who's Made $30 Million Has Already Started Working on His Next Career—Chicken Farmer," *Business Insider*, February 1, 2016, http://www.businessinsider.com/ von-miller-raises-chickens-for-future-chicken-farm-2016-2.

13   Scott Dinsmore, "57 Living Legends Expose the Moment that Defined their Passion," *Live Your Legend*, July 27, 2011, http:// liveyourlegend.net/57-online-rockstars-expose-how-they-crushed -fear-to-succeed/.

14   T. S. Eliot, *Knowledge and Experience in the Philosophy of F.H. Bradley* (New York: Columbia University Press, 1989), Chapter 1.

15 Passion Stories interview with Peter Sims, "Peter Sims, Writer and Entrepreneur," *Passion Stories*, November 9, 2014, http://www .passionstories.co/writing/peter-sims-writer-and-entrepreneur.

16 James Clear, "How Creative Geniuses Come Up with Great Ideas," http://jamesclear.com/markus-zusak.

17 Anne Lamott, *Bird by Bird: Some Instructions on Writing and Life* (New York: Anchor, 1994).

## CHAPTER 2

1 Jenna Arak, "Overcoming the Fear of Not Being Good Enough," *The Everygirl*, http://theeverygirl.com/overcoming-the-fear-of-not -being-good-enough.

2 Neel Burton, "What Are Basic Emotions?," *Psychology Today*, January 7, 2016, https://www.psychologytoday.com/blog/hide-and -seek/201601/what-are-basic-emotions.

3 Julia La Roche, "Kyle Bass: 'I Live with This Constant Feeling of Inadequacy,'" *Business Insider*, February 9, 2015, http://www .businessinsider.com/kyle-bass-interview-on-real-vision-tv-2015 -2#ixzz3bSOWVsgw.

4 Walter Isaacson, *Steve Jobs* (New York: Simon & Schuster, 2011).

5 Bob Samples, *The Metaphoric Mind: A Celebration of Creative Consciousness* (Reading, MA: Addison-Wesley Pub. Co., 1976).

6 University of Leeds, "Go with Your Gut—Intuition Is More Than Just a Hunch, Says Leeds Research," 2008, http://www.leeds.ac .uk/news/article/367/go_with_your_gut-intuition_is_more_than _just_a_hunch_says_leeds_research.

7    P. Lally, C. H. M. Van Jaarsveld, H. W. W. Potts, and J. Wardle
     (2009). "How Are Habits Formed: Modelling Habit Formation in
     the Real World," *European Journal of Social Psychology*, http://
     repositorio.ispa.pt/bitstream/10400.12/3364/1/IJSP_998-1009.pdf.

8    Brené Brown, *The Gifts of Imperfection: Let Go of Who You Think
     You're Supposed to Be and Embrace Who You Are* (Center City, MN:
     Hazelden Publishing, 2010).

9    Teja Ravilochan, "A 30-Second Story to Remember When You Feel
     Inadequate," *Unreasonable*, December 30, 2013, http://unreasonable
     .is/a-30-second-story-to-remember-when-you-feel-inadequate/.

10   K. Dickinson, T. Jankot, and H. Gracon, 2009, "Sun Mentoring:
     1996–2009," http://spcoast.com/pub/Katy/SunMentoring1996
     -2009.smli_tr-2009-185.pdf.

11   Chris Guillebeau, "The No-Fear Legacy," *Fear.less Magazine*,
     June 2010, https://www.scribd.com/document/32720045/
     Fear-lessJUNE2010.

## CHAPTER 3

1    Nick Bilton, "Disruptions: Innovation Isn't Easy, Especially
     Midstream," *Bits, New York Times*, April 15, 2012, http://bits
     .blogs.nytimes.com/2012/04/15/disruptions-innovation-isnt-easy
     -especially-midstream/?_r=0.

2    E. A. Locke, K. N. Shaw, L. M. Saari, and G. P. Latham (July
     1981). "Goal Setting and Task Performance: 1969–1980,"
     *Psychological Bulletin*, Vol. 90 (1), 125–52, http://psycnet.apa.org/
     psycinfo/1981-27276-001.

3    Jim Asplund and Nikki Blacksmith, "Embedding Strengths in Your
     Company's DNA," Gallup, June 12, 2012, http://www.gallup.com/
     businessjournal/155036/embedding-strengths-company-dna.aspx.

4    Hallie Golden, "EPA CIO Wants Her Tech Team to Take Smart
     Risks," Nextgov, June 9, 2015, http://www.nextgov.com/cio-briefing
     /2015/06/epas-ann-dunkin-wants-her-technology-team-take-smart
     -risks/114871/.

5    Bud Bilanich, "50 Famous People Who Failed at Their First
     Attempt at Career Success," http://www.budbilanich.com/50
     -famous-people-who-failed-at-their-first-attempt-at-career-success/.

## CHAPTER 4

1    F. L. Dyer and T. C. Martin, *Edison: His Life and Inventions* (New
     York: Harper & Brothers, 1910).

2    Ilan Mochari, "Try, Try Again: Lessons from James Dyson's
     Invention of the Vacuum," *Inc.*, August 14, 2014, http://www
     .inc.com/ilan-mochari/vacuum-innovation.html.

3    Shahrzad Rafati, "Why It's Okay to Make Mistakes at Work,"
     Fortune.com, March 31, 2015, http://fortune.com/2015/03/31/
     shahrzad-rafati-best-mistake/.

4    H. M. Sisti, A. L. Glass, and T. J. Shors (2007). "Neurogenesis and
     the Spacing Effect: Learning Over Time Enhances Memory and the
     Survival of New Neurons," *Learning & Memory* 14(5): 368–75.

5    Ferris Jabr, "Why Your Brain Needs More Downtime," *Scientific
     American*, October 15, 2013, http://www.scientificamerican.com/
     article/mental-downtime/.

6    Travis Bradberry, "How Cutthroat Work Cultures Suck the Life
     Out of You," LinkedIn, September 19, 2016, http://www.linkedin.
     com/pulse/how-cutthroat-work-cultures-suck-life-out-you-dr-travis
     -bradberry.


## CHAPTER 5

1    Roald Dahl, *My Uncle Oswald* (New York: Knopf, 1980).

2    Marguerite Ward, "This Biz Bounced Back from Near Failure to
     Sell Over 1 Million Products," CNBC, May 25, 2016, http://www
     .cnbc.com/2016/05/25/this-biz-bounced-back-from-near-failure-to
     -sell-over-1-million-products.html.


## CHAPTER 6

1    Samantha Murphy, "Report: 56% of Social Media Users Suffer from
     FOMO," *Mashable*, July 9, 2013, http://mashable.com/
     2013/07/09/fear-of-missing-out/#By6ZsiOMlaqS.

2    Twyla Tharp and Mark Reiter, *The Creative Habit: Learn It and Use
     It for Life: A Practical Guide* (New York: Simon & Schuster, 2003).

3    Mary MacVean, "For Many People, Gathering Possessions Is Just
     the Stuff of Life," *Los Angeles Times*, March 21, 2014, http://articles
     .latimes.com/2014/mar/21/health/la-he-keeping-stuff-20140322.

4    M. Smith, L. Robinson, and R. Segal (2017). "How Much Sleep
     Do We Really Need?," *HelpGuide*, http://www.helpguide.org/
     articles/sleep/how-much-sleep-do-you-need.htm.

## CHAPTER 7

1   Minda Zetlin, Inc., "Steve Jobs Asked Himself One Question Every Day—and You Should, Too," *Business Insider*, August 5, 2015, http://www.businessinsider.com/steve-jobs-asked-himself-one -question-every-day-and-you-should-too-2015-8?utm_content =bufferb8c96&utm_medium=social&utm_source=facebook.com &utm_campaign=buffer.

2   Scott Schieman, Paul Glavin, and Melissa Milkie (2009). "When Work Interferes with Life: Work-Nonwork Interference and the Influence of Work-Related Demands and Resources," *American Sociological Review*, Vol. 74 (6), 966–87.

3   Alain de Botton, 2015, twitter.com, https://twitter.com/alainde botton/status/590968878798352385.

4   R. E. Silverman, "Jack Welch: 'No Such Thing as Work-Life Balance,'" The Juggle, *Wall Street Journal*, July 13, 2009, http:// blogs.wsj.com/juggle/2009/07/13/jack-welch-no-such-thing-as -work-life-balance/.

5   S. Sandberg, Makers.com, 2017, *The Success/Likeability Tradeoff*, http://www.makers.com/moments/successlikeability-tradeoff.

6   Heather Schuck, *The Working Mom Manifesto* (United States: Voyager Media, 2013).

7   Michael Thomas Sunnarborg, *21 Keys to Work/Life Balance: Unlock Your Full Potential*, edited by Beth Wallace and Elizabeth Frick (United States: Michael Thomas Sunnarborg, 2013).

## CHAPTER 8

1   Darcy Andries, *The Secret of Success Is Not a Secret* (Portland, ME: Sellers Pub, 2008).

2   Sarah Landrum, "How Strict Working Hours Can Hinder Productivity," Women 2.0, October 14, 2015, http://women2.com/ stories/2015/10/14/strict-working-hours.

3   Ted Goodman, ed. *Forbes Book of Quotations: 10,000 Thoughts on the Business of Life* (New York: Black Dog & Leventhal, 2016).

4   Jonah Lehrer, "Brainstorming: An Idea Past Its Prime," *Washington Post*, April 19, 2012, https://www.washingtonpost.com/opinions/ brainstorming-an-idea-past-its-prime/2012/04/19/gIQAhKT5TT _story.html?utm_term=.ba99d39f505b.

5   Mousumi Saha Kumar, "John Stephen Akhwari: The Greatest Last Place Finish in the Olympic History," BrainPrick, July 19, 2012, http://brainprick.com/john-stephen-akhwari-the-greatest-last-place -finish-in-olympic-history/.


## CHAPTER 9

1   Marie Forleo, "How to Get Over the Fear of Being Judged by Others," http://www.marieforleo.com/2011/11/fear-of-being-judged/.

2   Maritz Research Hospitality Group 2011 Employee Engagement Poll, 2011, http://www.maritz.com/~/media/Files/MaritzDotCom/ White%20Papers/ExcecutiveSummary_Research.ashx.

3   *McKinsey Quarterly* interview with Kevin Sharer, "Why I'm a Listener: Amgen CEO Kevin Sharer," McKinsey & Company,

2012, http://www.mckinsey.com/global-themes/leadership/why-im
-a-listener-amgen-ceo-kevin-sharer.

4    D. S. Viscott, *Finding Your Strength in Difficult Times: A Book of
Meditations* (Chicago: Contemporary Books, 1993).

5    Fred Howard, *Wilbur and Orville: A Biography of the Wright Brothers*
(Mineola, NY: Dover Publications, 1998).

6    Jennifer Robison, interview with Sangeeta Badal, "Why So Many
New Companies Fail During Their First Five Years," Gallup,
October 23, 2014, http://www.gallup.com/businessjournal/178787/
why-new-companies-fail-during-first-five-years.aspx.

## CHAPTER 10

1    Annie Dillard, *Teaching a Stone to Talk* (New York: Harper Collins,
1988).

2    Micah Solomon, "Entrepreneurs: Should You Quit Your Day Job?
We Ask Shark Tank's Daymond John," *Inc.*, June 29, 2015, http://
www.inc.com/micah-solomon/when-should-an-entrepreneur-quit
-their-day-job-shark tank-s-daymond-john-has-the.html.

3    "Stress Is Killing You," graphic from MastersDegreeOnline.org,
American Institute of Stress, http://www.stress.org/stress-is-killing
-you/.

## CHAPTER 11

1   Suzanne Styles, "10 Steps to Overcoming the Shame and Guilt of Failure," LinkedIn, August 31, 2015, http://www.linkedin.com/pulse/10-steps-overcoming-shame-guilt-failure-suzanne-styles.

2   James Burke, *Connections* (Boston: Little, Brown and Company, 1978).

3   Stephen Schaefer, "Billy Crystal's 'Monster' Regret," ABC News, November 1, 2001, http://abcnews.go.com/Entertainment/story?id=101549&page=1.

4   "90 Percent of People Say They Have a Major Regret. Here's How to Move Past It," *Huffington Post*, graphic from Happify.com, June 6, 2014, http://www.huffingtonpost.com/2014/06/26/regret-infographic_n_5529641.html.

# ABOUT THE AUTHOR

ADAM KIRK SMITH is an entrepreneur, consultant, and public speaker. His popular blog, asmithblog.com, offers insights on leadership, bravery, and life purpose, among other topics. Named one of the most influential people of 2014 by *American Genius*, Smith has written for *Entrepreneur* and *Success Magazine*, among others, and has been featured in *Newsday* and other media. He lives in Illinois with his family.

You can connect with Adam by e-mail at adam@asmithblog.com or on social media at the links below:

> twitter.com/asmithblog
> facebook.com/asmithblog
> instagram.com/asmithblog
> linkedin.com/in/asmithblog
> youtube.com/asmithblog